WHO ARE GOD'S PEOPLE IN THE MIDDLE EAST?

The Lord's Prayer in Arabic
Used by Palestinian Christians throughout Israel/Palestine

WHO ARE GOD'S PEOPLE IN THE MIDDLE EAST?

GARY M. BURGE

ZondervanPublishingHouse
Academic and Professional Books
Grand Rapids, Michigan

A Division of HarperCollinsPublishers

Requests for information should be addressed to:
Zondervan Publishing House
Academic and Professional Books
Grand Rapids, Michigan 49530

Unless otherwise noted, all Scripture citations are taken from the *New Revised Standard Version of the Bible*, copyright © 1989 by the Division of Christian Education of the National Council of the Churches of Christ in the United States of America.

Edited by Verlyn D. Verbrugge and Laura Weller
Cover design by Jack Foster Design
Maps by Louise Bauer

Library of Congress Cataloging-in-Publication Data

Burge, Gary M., 1952–
    Who are God's people in the Middle East? / Gary M. Burge.
        p.   cm.
    Includes index.
    ISBN 0-310-38691-8
    1. Jewish-Arab relations. 2. Bible—Prophecies—Israel. 3. Christians—Israel. I. Title.
DS119.7.B83   1993   93-11235
261.8'7'095694—dc20.   CIP

Printed in the United States of America

93 94 95 96 97 98 / DH / 10 9 8 7 6 5 4 3 2 1

To My Parents

*Who generously and courageously sent me
to Beirut, Lebanon, in 1972
as a university student.*

Those days have left their mark.

Let me sing for my beloved
    my love-song concerning his vineyard:
My beloved had a vineyard
    on a very fertile hill.
He dug it and cleared it of stones,
    and planted it with choice vines;
he built a watchtower in the midst of it,
    and hewed out a wine vat in it;
he expected it to yield grapes,
    but it yielded wild grapes.

And now, inhabitants of Jerusalem
    and people of Judah,
judge between me
    and my vineyard.
What more was there to do for my vineyard
    that I have not done in it?
When I expected it to yield grapes,
    why did it yield wild grapes?

                          (Isaiah 5:1–4)

CONTENTS

INTRODUCTION

"Whoever walks four cubits in the Land of Israel is assured of a place in the world to come." (T. B. Kethuboth 110b–111a)

At the height of the Gulf War in January 1991, Dr. John Walvoord, formerly president of Dallas Seminary, was being interviewed on Moody Radio in Chicago. While American warplanes were attacking Saddam Hussein's forces in Iraq and Kuwait, Dr. Walvoord spoke eloquently about Bible prophecy and its fulfillment in the modern Middle East.

It was an exciting and compelling presentation. Could this configuration of Arab and Western armies spell the beginning of the countdown that would end history? In 1948 Israel had returned to its ancient homeland and reestablished its nationhood—an astonishing twentieth-century miracle. Some orthodox Jewish groups in Jerusalem were even talking about rebuilding the temple. The puzzle pieces were coming together. As short-range Scud missiles landed in Tel Aviv, many Bible-believing Christians echoed Dr. Walvoord's sentiments as they studied Ezekiel, Daniel, and the book of Revelation, searching for clues to help decipher each day's newspaper headlines. Perhaps Armageddon was around the corner. Some were even calling Hussein the Antichrist.

It was easy to get caught up in that enthusiasm. In fact, just before the outbreak of hostilities, many of us cheered the prospect of war. *If war means that the second coming of Jesus is approaching, then let the fighting begin! If war means that the eschatological clock will tick a little faster, so be it.* Not only were we on the winning side militarily, but we knew that the host of heaven would be drawn into the action soon.

But then we saw something disturbing. A laser guided bomb plowed directly into a bomb shelter and incinerated hundreds of Iraqi children and women hiding there. Reports after the war described that our carpet bombing of the front with B-52s may have destroyed over 100,000 Iraqi lives. That's 100,000 people! Many were men and boys who had no desire whatsoever to be there. Saddam's elite troops had gone elsewhere. As the allies moved forward, Iraqi soldiers surrendered eagerly. They were conscripts, many of whom were kept in their bunkers on threat of death. Mine fields were laid behind them (to keep them from fleeing) as well as in front of them. By the war's end, about 115,000 Iraqi soldiers died, 3000 Arab civilians died in the air war, and almost 120,000 civilians died after the cease fire from civil unrest or war-related ailments.[1] In a word, the war completely destroyed the Iraqi infrastructure. This has led many to question whether or not the war fulfilled what once was called a "just war." At the time of writing, masses of Iraqi children (500 per day under the age of five by some estimates) were still dying from the war's delayed effects.[2]

In light of the outcome of the war, I have had to ask myself some hard questions. *Did I have room in my heart for the suffering that this war created? Was my commitment to eschatology greater than my commitment to these people whom God surely loved?* I could not justify or excuse the ruthless and unpardonable Iraqi conquest of Kuwait. But something had happened to me. My eschatological zeal, my fervor to see prophecy fulfilled, had made me stereotype the Arabs, making them pawns in some game I was playing with my faith and my Bible. I was in a dilemma.

Many of us in the evangelical community live with a troubled conscience.[3] We are learning that our vision is not what it should be. Our excitement at living in "the last days" and our ready support of Israel has led us to overlook some devastating facts about our faith, the Middle East, and what God would have us do. In some cases, we have not been told things, important things, about life as it really is in the Middle East.

As an evangelical Christian, as a professor of New Testament, as a pastor, Israel and the Middle East confront me with an impossible problem. How do I embrace my commitment to Judaism, a commitment to which I am bound by the New Testament, when I sense in my deepest being that there is a profound injustice afoot in Israel? How do I celebrate the birth of this nation Israel when I also mourn the suffering of Arab Christians who are equally my brothers and sisters in Christ? And how do I love those Palestinian Muslims who are deeply misunderstood by all parties in this conflict?

This small book is not written for the academic historian or the technically trained theologian, although its conclusions and observations are based on many academic works. This book is practical. It is written for the average Christian who, like me, struggles on a basic personal level with the dilemma of Israel and the Palestinians within an evangelical theological framework.

Discerning readers will at once see that this book has been a personal exploration of my own. In it I have tried to explore and distill the essential ideas that we must acknowledge if we are to understand Israel fully. Some will quickly look to see "where I come from": Is he pro-Israeli or pro-Palestinian? I am as comfortable in an Arab *service* taxi in Husseini Square, Nablus, as I am riding an Israeli Egged bus out of Tel Aviv's Central Bus Station. I have slept in Gaza City as well as in Israeli West Bank settlements. Hopefully, such readers will patiently and thoughtfully weigh the evidence as I have done and discover that grave problems lie within Israel/Palestine.

Chapter 1 is an introduction to the problem of Israel/ Palestine from a very personal point of view. In it I outline the inquiries that follow in the rest of the book.

Throughout the book I have been careful in my use of words that are loaded with special meanings. Virtually everything—from the color of one's license plate to one's address—has some political meaning in Israel/Palestine. The same is true of vocabulary. For example, I use "Israel/Palestine" when referring to the larger country which includes the lands occupied in the 1967 war (particularly the West Bank and Gaza). This term respects both peoples' desire for national identity. Palestine is an ancient word that has been used since Roman times to describe this land.[4] And today Palestinian has become the preferred title of the people who live there. When I refer to Israel or Israeli, I generally mean the Jewish nation formed in 1948.

Many people contributed to the writing of this book, and I want to render thanks where it is due. The bulk of my research, travel, and writing took place at North Park College during a 1992 sabbatical. North Park's board of trustees; its president, David Horner; and my dean, Dean Ebner, all deserve thanks. North Park's urban setting and its full commitment to the issues of the world have challenged and encouraged me to pursue issues such as this one. Dorothy-Ellen Gross, Sonia Bodi, and Norma Sutton, professional librarians at North Park, provided research facilities and tremendous assistance. Other friends gave advice and assistance as the project developed. Many helped me organize interviews in Israel/Palestine itself. Special thanks are due to Don Wagner, Ken Bailey, Peter Kapenga, and Rosemary and Herman Ruether.

Many friends in Israel/Palestine invited me to enter their world in a way that few visitors have opportunity to experience. They trusted me. And for this trust I cannot express enough appreciation. They are Naim and Maha Ateek (Jerusalem), Selwa Diabis (Ramallah), Bishara Awad (Bethlehem), Audeh and Pat Rantisi (Ramallah), Zoughbi Elias Zoughbi (Jerusalem), Salim Munayer (Bethlehem), Riah Abu El Assal (Nazareth), Saleem Zaru (Ramallah), Amin Abu Hanna (manager at St. Margaret's Hospice, Nazareth), Nadia Abboushi (Ramallah), and Inam Bonoura (Beit Sahour). I also want to thank the warden at Ahli Arab Hospital in Gaza City for opening the gate for me while Israelis and Palestinians were exchanging stones, tear gas, and bullets on the street. It was not a good day for visitors.

A special thank you goes to my wife, Carol, who has generously encouraged me to make so many trips to Israel/Palestine. Her support has helped me pursue this issue for many years. Ashley and Grace, our daughters, have become accustomed to asking, "When will Daddy be home from the Middle East?"

NOTES

1. *Newsweek*, January 20, 1992, 18. *Newsweek*'s sources came from the Department of Defense, the U.S. Central Command, the U.S.

Intelligence Agencies, and Greenpeace, USA. These figures compare with 305 American troops killed (146 killed in action, 159 killed outside combat) and 244 casualties among the other allied armies.

2. Charles Scriven, "Second Thoughts About the War," *Christianity Today*, January 13, 1992, 11.

3. D. Neff, "Love Thy (Arab) Neighbor." *Christianity Today*, October 22, 1990, 22. Neff writes, "When international disputes escalate to this extent, the church has a special responsibility to douse the flames of hatred."

4. In fact, *Palestine* goes back further. It originates with the word *Philistine*, which occurs throughout the Old Testament.

Part One
The Question of the Land

Chapter One

THE DILEMMA
OF ISRAEL/PALESTINE

"Blessed are the meek, for they will inherit the earth; . . .
Blessed are the peacemakers, for they will be called children
of God." (Matt. 5:5, 9)

Certain memories remain fixed in the imagination. They
are personal, and they become indelible symbols as they help
us to understand what transpired in our past. Each of us lives
with an archive of such memories, and occasionally we redraw
those landscapes, we reconstruct those conversations and
crises, making them seem as though they happened yesterday.
In some fashion, their power is still with us.

LEBANON, 1973

I was an exchange student in Beirut, Lebanon, in the early
1970s during the outbreak of the Lebanese civil war. Palestinian
refugees who had lost their homes in Israel lived in squalid
camps around Beirut, and they had upset the uneasy balance of
Lebanon's politics. The year I was at the American University of
Beirut, the Lebanese army had begun its fight with these
Palestinian camps, and from the balcony of my dormitory I
could watch French Mirage jets strafing the refugee camps less
than three miles away. One lead fighter would shriek downward with its partner close behind. If the first plane drew the

aim of the antiaircraft gunner, the first pilot would pull out of his approach while the second jet attacked with awesome ferocity. The roar was deafening. And when the bombs made impact, the rumble vibrated through our building. We would sit, eating pita bread, tuna fish and Arabic hummus (a chickpea and garlic purée) on the sixth-floor balconies of the dorm on Bliss Street as if we were watching an arcade game.

The Palestinian students on my floor were crazed with anger. How could an army destroy civilians like this? When the angry students started throwing furniture out of the dorm windows into the busy street below, the Lebanese army rolled a tank up Bliss Street and parked it one-half block away, aiming its barrel at the top floors of the dorm. It was tough even to get a peek at the thing. A squad of soldiers fired hardened rubber bullets at anyone who showed his or her profile in a window. We slept at night with wet towels crammed under the door of our room to keep the tear gas out. My Palestinian roommate, Samir El Far, made it his mission to keep this naive American out of harm's way. We spent the days and nights talking about what these things meant.

Since college classes usually do not prosper under such circumstances—the furniture from one of my classrooms had been taken to form a barricade—most of us thought it would be good to get away. I joined a teacher and a busload of students and headed south into the beautiful, rolling hills of southern Lebanon. Our destination was the village of Hesbiya. Palestinians fleeing the war in Beirut and Palestinians wishing to return to their homeland in Israel were settling in southern Lebanon not far from the Israeli border. Many had become guerilla fighters in their own right, some were simply gangsters, but most were families living in abject confusion, wandering from place to place.

The Israelis had plans for southern Lebanon as well. They wanted to depopulate it, to drive the Palestinians away from Israel's northern border, so they sent fighter jets into these hills to attack the Palestinians. In the process, they attacked any Lebanese village that gave refuge to the Palestinian refugees.[1]

When we entered Hesbiya, I saw firsthand the results of a fresh F-16 attack: the crumbled buildings, the panic, and the dismay. I remember seeing brightly colored children's toys locked under the weight of massive broken concrete blocks. The misshapen steel reinforcement rods stuck into the air like arms reaching nowhere. The toys were red and plastic, and I wondered where the children were who played with them. Kids were everywhere telling us in indecipherable Arabic and hand gestures how the jets swooped down on them firing. These kids saw themselves as heroes. Bravado was on their little faces. They had survived.

We had come to build a bomb shelter for Hesbiya. Before we finished the foundation, a village elder slaughtered a chicken (for some reason) to bless the structure. Then stone upon stone, we constructed the walls of the underground shelter. The people mainly wanted a place for the children to hide when the jets returned. And they did return many times later after we left. I often wonder what became of that shelter and how it fared in those days of attack.

In the span of just a few weeks I witnessed the crisis of the Palestinian world. Attacked by the Lebanese, attacked by the Israelis, these people had nowhere to go. They were becoming the refuse of Middle Eastern history. They were of no use to anyone. I remember walking in the hills outside the village at night. It was very dark and very quiet. The stars seemed crowded in this sky that didn't suffer from the light pollution of my native Southern California. God seemed very near to this place. And yet it was a place of tragedy beyond description.

ISRAEL, 1990

In the following eighteen years I returned to the Middle East many times: sometimes as a pilgrim, frequently as a professor with students, and often as a researcher hoping to understand more of this turbulent world. I found a profound dilemma.

This was a land of miracles. This was the Holy Land—the land of Abraham, Moses, and Jesus. This was a place that witnessed the miraculous rebirth of the nation of Israel, surely a triumph that has no parallel elsewhere in history. Once after reading Hal Lindsey's *Late Great Planet Earth* I stood in the

Valley of Armageddon and reflected on Israel's fulfillment of prophecy and the coming wars that would torment these lands and bring about the end of human history as we know it. Surely God was at work in this place.

But I also witnessed suffering and sinfulness in an unprecedented way. Both Arab evil and Israeli evil abounded. Whenever I left the usual tourist trail and looked behind the scenes, I caught glimpses of an Israel I barely recognized.

I was in Israel/Palestine in 1990 visiting an Arabic Christian pastor and his family. This pastor's home had become a refuge for many who sought support and protection. At 7:00 in the morning an elderly Palestinian woman burst into the kitchen where we were eating breakfast. Her story riveted us. The Israeli army had come that night to homes on her street looking for stone-throwing boys. It was about midnight, and the children were in bed. In panic they fled as soldiers with weapons tore through the bedrooms. Zena, a twelve-year-old girl, fled out the front door and there on the porch was shot point blank by a soldier with an automatic weapon. She was barely alive.

The woman fell to the floor, and her weeping—her incessant weeping—paralyzed us all. I knew what she was talking about. Just the day before I had been walking up Al Tireh Street, Ramallah's main boulevard, and there watched a platoon of soldiers shake down a row of homes. An officer told me that a child had thrown a rock out of the yard and it had hit the new car of an Israeli settler. Now the soldiers were looking for him. They could find only women and young children since school was in session and the men were away at work. The residents were told to line up in the field in front of the houses while the soldiers searched more carefully. I squatted down next to a jeep, watching in amazement. A girl of about five ran into the street, her mother screamed as she pursued her, and the soldiers yelled for them to get back in line. Then the rocks started falling. Soldiers on the top of the buildings nearby started targeting the young woman and her child with apple-sized stones. It was their laughter that disturbed me; it was their grisly sport here in Ramallah that I found stunning. The young mother swept up her child with tears streaming down her face and fled for the cover of trees. And there she wept. To this day I can still see and hear her weeping in the trees of Ramallah.

I deduced what happened next. The frustrated platoon decided to come back that night and in a surprise raid catch whomever they could. The young critically wounded girl was just one more accidental victim.

We returned to breakfast, and the Palestinian Christian pastor said grace in a way I will never forget: "Lord, thank you for this food you give us this day. And please Lord remember those of us who suffer in this land and remember to bring justice to us."

It was time to leave Ramallah. I joined a communal taxi already filled with Arab riders and headed south toward Jerusalem. I climbed out of the taxi on the Nablus Road just north of the Old City's Damascus Gate. I bought a popsicle from a vendor, and as I watched, an army patrol stopped its truck on the road in front of me and began to abuse the passengers in the waiting cars. They were the dreaded Border Regiments that work primarily in the occupied territories and are known for their forest green berets and their bravado. I watched as soldiers reached into the windows of the filled taxis and slapped people across the face. My anger was brimming—I had been with these people; my car had Arab medical students in it. But I had an overwhelming sense of powerlessness. I did not know how to control my rage at the injustice, the provocation.

Cameras are always a fierce weapon before soldiers, so I loaded mine, slipped off the lens cap, and rested it on my chest provocatively. At once the patrol spotted me, the only blonde in a sea of Arab faces. With clubs poised inches from me they screamed in Hebrew something about photos. It was surreal. There I was standing face to face with a squad of heavily armed, arrogant young men. Each had a white-knuckled grip on his club and had weapons loaded with live clips. It became very clear that this was going to be one of the most expensive rolls of film I had ever tried to shoot!

Compassion is a Latin word that means "to suffer with." I had crossed an invisible yet tangible line somewhere. Deep

within me fear and courage were at work. For a moment I was
sure I wanted to be arrested. To confront the system. To dare
them to do to an American citizen what they were doing to
these people.

Suddenly a Russian Israeli officer approached, intervened
by yelling at the men, and escorted the squad back to the truck.
Palestinian faces everywhere were looking at me—from the
taxis to the sidewalk crowds. I turned to look at a shopkeeper
behind me, and he smiled a smile like no other—a smile of
grace, of sorrow, and of thanks—as the Israelis drove off. All I
could say, as if he represented his entire people, was, "I'm
sorry." And I walked on into the old city of Jerusalem.

Inside the Damascus Gate I could tell that a demonstration
was about to erupt. Shops were slamming closed and people
were running. Israeli patrols had mounted the high walls
surrounding the gate, and they were distributing tear-gas
canisters and locking them on to the underside of their rifle
barrels. About seventy-five teenage girls packed a narrow street
in that quarter of Jerusalem chanting and clapping. An Arab
shopkeeper grabbed me, saying that it was not good for me to
stay there, but I felt compelled, intoxicated by the surge of
voices and curious to witness the fate that awaited them. A
patrol of soldiers—I could see them—was about four hundred
yards ahead. The girls sang as men in sunglasses loaded and
aimed tear-gas guns, M-16s, and Uzi machine guns. There was
a scream, gas, panic, a stampede, and retching. The girls
retreated from their demonstration as I sprinted up an alley to
get away from the gas.

My head was still swimming from the adrenalin. I needed
a place to sort out my feelings, to clear out my thinking. I
followed a small road called the El Wad going south and then
headed east on the Via Dolorosa, the Way of Suffering walked
by Jesus as he headed toward the cross of Golgotha. It was also
the street where the women of Jerusalem wept for him. I knew
of a private place—a quiet place, a place to settle down—and
was anxious to weave through the crowds to get there. For a
shekel the Sisters of Zion (a Catholic order) will let you into the
remains of the ancient Roman Antonia Fortress. There underground, beneath the streets of Jerusalem, in perfect solitude,

are pavements and cisterns built by the Romans to equip the Roman occupation army of the first century. The deepest ladder took me far from the awful world above. And there it hit me like nothing before: I was sitting amid the ruins of the Roman army that terrorized and battered this land in Jesus' day. An army that Jesus knew all too well. An army that slapped him and crucified him and killed him.

So it had been Jesus' experience too. Did he feel what I felt? Did his followers not want him to do more? And I wept for the first time since I had visited this land.

FOUR COMPLICATIONS

Why is it that we sense we cannot get anywhere when it comes to Israel and the Palestinians? Why have Christians been peculiarly—and sometimes rightly—paralyzed when it comes to this subject? Passions always flare when someone brings up aid for Israel or the settlement of the West Bank or the Palestinian Intifada. It seems to me that four factors continue to influence and complicate our thoughts:

1. We bear a subliminal sense of guilt for the horrors of the twentieth century that have been perpetrated on Judaism. We share the guilt of men and women who, in the name of Christ, pursued, persecuted, and massacred Jews. From Moscow to Chicago, anti-Semitism is a part of the heritage of Western Christendom. Jews were killed by the Byzantine armies, the Holy Roman Empire, and even the Crusaders. When the Crusaders entered Jerusalem in A.D. 1099 in the name of Christ, they massacred everyone who looked Middle Eastern, Muslims and Jews alike. Few in the Middle East have forgotten this.

And twentieth-century Jews have had to face similar horrors. It is no accident, for instance, that our Jewish neighbors' synagogues all around my college in Chicago have metal fireproof doors on their buildings. They can often be seen scrubbing off swastikas from the alleyway entrances. Kristall-nacht, the night of November 9, 1938, commemorates the day when the Nazi SS began destroying Jewish businesses and synagogues in Munich. Its anniversary is still remembered each year, especially in Skokie, north of Chicago, among the neo-Nazis. Jews in the synagogues there pray that the night will pass without incident.

And so our relationship with Israel is complicated by a collective feeling of guilt. These people have suffered severely in history, and our debt to their future is great. Judaism deserves a place of security—a place to protect itself from outsiders. I cannot imagine the restraint it took for the Israelis not to respond with force when Saddam Hussein was lobbing Scud missiles at Tel Aviv in early 1990. "To defend yourself and not rely on someone else's guns" is a vow that was born somewhere in the Warsaw ghetto in the 1930s. I recall standing on the top of the mountain of Masada, the "last stand" of the Jews against the Romans. And there I watched the bar mitzvah of a young man in the ruins of the two-thousand-year-old synagogue. As he vowed in the silence of the desert to embrace his faith and his land with his entire life, an F-16 fighter barreling down the Jordan Valley screamed defiantly over the mountain and its synagogue with a deafening roar. Judaism will never be desecrated in a ghetto again. Ever. And this is good.

2. Evangelical Christians have rightly concluded that we of all people have a shared sense of spiritual destiny with Judaism. Our branches spring from the same Middle Eastern olive tree. We share a parallel faith. The Lord is the same God both of synagogue and church. Every autumn thousands of evangelical Christians flood into Jerusalem from the United States and Europe to celebrate the Festival of Tabernacles. They march around the walled city of Jerusalem arm-in-arm with Jewish worshipers, waving palms and praising God for the harvest of vine and tree. Teddy Kollek, Jerusalem's mayor, gives a speech praising the evangelicals' presence.

We know that Jesus was Jewish. He was of the tribe of Judah, a descendant of David. Paul was from the tribe of Benjamin, a rabbi. Eighty percent of our Bible belongs to the Hebrew canon. The Lord's Supper is actually a Jewish Passover Seder. And above all, we are commanded in Scripture to bless the children in Abraham. Paul's life witnessed intense hostility from the Jewish synagogues: he was jailed, cursed, arrested, flogged with forty lashes five times, beaten with rods three times, and nearly stoned to death once. And still he could say (in Romans 11) that for the sake of the promises God made to their ancestors, the Jewish people—especially those who refuse to believe in Christ—are still beloved (Rom. 11:28). Judaism holds an incomparable place in divine history.

And so our relationship with Israel is further complicated by the kinship we feel with this Israeli state that overtly professes faith in the God of Jesus. Even the Israeli Parliament building (called the Knesset) is architecturally designed to recall the Ten Commandments—ostensibly the basis of secular Jewish law. Christians can only wish that our American Supreme Court could do as well.

3. Deep within our instincts we have concluded that we are witnesses to a miracle in the twentieth century. The nation of Israel is God's doing. The return of the Jews to Israel after 2000 years, Israel's survival against inestimable odds—are these not signs of something larger than history? How many cultures alive today are 3,500 years old, have suffered multiple exiles, and then after 2000 years of assimilation into the European world have resurrected their dead language and life in a self-sustaining state?

After the miraculous Israeli victory in 1967's Six-Day War, evangelical Christians throughout America and Europe were freely and confidently exclaiming that God had stepped in and won the victory on behalf of the Israeli defense forces. Legends circulated widely from one Christian pulpit to the next of besieged Israeli soldiers whose Arab enemies were quickly closing in on them with overwhelming firepower. Then suddenly there was a reversal of fortune—was it an angelic army?—and the Arab soldiers retreated in droves. Clearly, many of us have claimed, this victory and the others—1948, 1956, 1973—were miracles. God was defending Israel.

And so as we look at Israel through this lens, we are cautious. If this little nation in the eastern Mediterranean is God's handiwork, if Israel's history is being orchestrated from on high, then we should be slow to criticize, careful about our chastisements, and supportive at all costs. Evangelicals are prone to cite Genesis 12:2–3 as a reasonable approach to Middle Eastern foreign policy. In this passage God says to Abraham, "I will make of you a great nation, and I will bless you, and make your name great, so that you will be a blessing. I will bless those who bless you, and the one who curses you I will curse; and in you all the families of the earth shall be blessed."

4. In 1991 we rediscovered the fourth factor that influences our judgments about Israel. At the height of the Gulf War suddenly it dawned on everyone that this might be the configuration of nations that will bring about the end of history. Hal Lindsay's *The Late Great Planet Earth* topped the 25 million mark in sales. John F. Walvoord's *Armageddon, Oil and the Middle East Crisis* now has 2 million copies in print thanks to the Gulf War. Both authors are saying the same thing: Israel will play a role in the end times. In fact, the hostility of the Arabs figures into a prophesied scenario in which Israel is backed up against the sea, total war breaks out in the Middle East, and Armageddon erupts, bringing about the end of human history as we know it today.

I heard a news commentator reflect on this idea one night in early January 1991 as American bombers were racing to Saudi Arabia. This announcer made the one deduction that was being pondered by evangelicals everywhere: If Armageddon is upon us, we had better be on the right side. No matter what happens militarily in the Middle East, evangelical eschatology demands that we keep a firm commitment to Israel. John Walvoord wrote during the Kuwait war, "The rise of military action in the Middle East [such as that taken by Iraq against Kuwait] is an important prophetic development. While wars in Korea, Vietnam, and Europe were not necessarily prophetically significant, all end-time prophecy pictures the Middle East as the center of political, financial, and military power at the end time."[2]

I receive a publication called "The Jerusalem Prayer Letter" distributed by an evangelical organization called Bridges for Peace. These are Christians who earnestly support Israel and work to foster Christian/Jewish understanding. Reflecting on the Gulf War, Jim Gerrish, the editor of the prayer letter, compared hostility against Israel during the war with the rise of Nebuchadnezzar in the Old Testament. Nebuchadnezzar, like Hussein, plotted the destruction of Jerusalem. Gerrish remarks:

> Today we now see presidents and nations taking their stand against the covenant people [Israel]. It would seem that all the odds are against Israel. Israel, however, has one thing in her favor. The King of the Universe is on her side and will remain so forever. It is Israel who will be the ultimate winner in any contest. Nations who come against her will vanish away (Psalm 129:6). Those who stand with her will be blessed both now and hereafter.[3]

And so when we look at Israel through this lens of eschatology, or prophecies of the end times, we are sobered. Sobered, lest we find ourselves playing on the wrong side of the table if the Lord should return during the next major conflict.

Together these four factors have made it difficult if not impossible to see Israel as just another nation. We have become paralyzed and perplexed, unable to launch appropriate criticisms of the Middle East. And just possibly, we have been unable to see other features of the land and its difficulties.

WHERE DO WE GO FROM HERE?

Many complicated technical works have given exhaustive attention to the problems of Israel/Palestine. Our goal will be to distill these works, decipher their leading arguments, and digest them as Christians might who have a heartfelt commitment to this Holy Land. As an evangelical writing to other evangelicals, I am hoping to make two simple points:

1. *If Israel makes a biblical claim to the land, then Israel must adhere to biblical standards of righteousness.* Land promises are a by-product of a covenant with God. And therefore all aspects of biblical nationhood must be at work. In chapters 2–6 we will examine what the Old Testament says about the land promises and how God's people should live on the land.

2. *Evangelicals must look more closely at their commitments.* The New Testament must be read alongside the Old Testament

when we interpret the land promises of the Bible. Further, Israel/Palestine has a body of Christian believers who today look to us for support. As fellow Christians we must ask if we have a spiritual obligation here as well. Chapters 7–11 give insights from the Palestinian Christian community.

An outline of each chapter and how it addresses these questions is given below:

Part 1: Understanding the Land

Chapter 2. We need to understand the land itself. What is its geography? Where is the West Bank? On what issues do the border disagreements focus? Why do the Palestinians fight against the "Israeli settlers"?

Part 2: The Old Testament and the Land

Chapter 3. What are the promises God has given concerning this land? Are the promises conditional? How does God's covenant connect with the land? Does the land ever belong to anyone, or is it always God's land?

Chapter 4. What obligation does the land bring to its occupier? Is the conquest of Joshua an apt parallel to the modern growth of the state of Israel? How did the Israelites treat non-Israelites (called aliens or sojourners)? Was the Old Testament kingdom of Israel an ethnically exclusive Jewish state?

Chapter 5. How do the prophets of the Old Testament relate the land of Israel to the people of Israel? What unique message did they bring? When they considered this inheritance, how did they explain Israel's loss of land during the exiles of the eighth and sixth centuries B.C.?

Chapter 6. Is the modern state of Israel claiming that there is a historical connection between biblical Israel and its own nationhood? If so, how do we apply the Old Testament to this modern nation? How does the modern state compare to Old Testament Israel?

Part 3: Christians and the Land

Chapter 7. Does the New Testament say anything about the land? What do Jesus and Paul say? If Christians are the descendants of Abraham by faith, what does this mean for the promises to Abraham's descendants?

Chapter 8. Who are the Palestinian Christians? What are their concerns? What have evangelicals not been told? What struggles do Palestinian Christians face?

Chapter 9. Who are the Palestinian Christian leaders whose voices need to be heard today? Who are some of the "silent saints" within the Palestinian church? What are they saying? What must evangelicals hear from them?

Chapter 10. How have Western evangelicals approached the question of Israel and the Palestinians? How should evangelicals relate to the Palestinian church? Should Israel be treated like "just any other nation"?

Epilogue. The epilogue brings many of the most recent developments into focus (e.g., the recent election of the Labor government and the current peace negotiations). It also asks, "Is it right to be critical of Israel? Is such criticism anti-Semitic?"

Appendix. The appendix has four poems from Palestine. The first, written by Kenneth E. Bailey, is a parable of the deep wound that bitterly divides this land. The other three are written by Hanan Mikhail-Ashrwi, professor of English at Bir Zeit University (Ramallah). This is the first time two of these poems have appeared in print.

NOTES

1. As I write (February 1992), the Israelis are engaged in a parallel campaign, fighting the radical pro-Iranian Palestinian groups in southern Lebanon. Numerous Israeli troops are well north of the frontier border.

2. John F. Walvoord, *Armageddon, Oil and the Middle East Crisis* (Grand Rapids: Zondervan, 1991), 48.

3. J. Gerrish, "Jerusalem Prayer Letter," November 18, 1991. Published by Bridges for Peace, Box 33145, Tulsa, OK 74153. Bridges for Peace also has an office in Jerusalem.

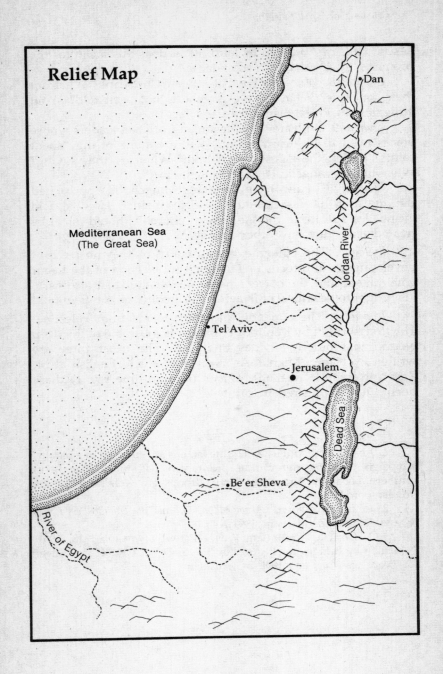

Relief Map

Mediterranean Sea
(The Great Sea)

Dan

Jordan River

Tel Aviv

Jerusalem

Dead Sea

Be'er Sheva

River of Egypt

Chapter Two

THE LAND

"The land that you are crossing over to occupy is a land of hills and valleys, watered by rain from the sky, a land that the LORD your God looks after. The eyes of the LORD your God are always on it from the beginning of the year to the end of the year." (Deut. 11:11–12)

The countryside of Israel is dotted with a series of peculiar-looking forts that date back to the British occupation of the country earlier this century. Tour guides generally pass by these since today they are outposts for the Israeli defense forces. They all have a distinctive architecture and are easy to identify. They were built by Sir Charles Teggart around 1937 and were used by the British to maintain control during the turbulent years before the founding of the modern state of Israel (1948). Teggart had come from India where he had a reputation for effective police enforcement. In Palestine he introduced a system of sixty-five military-police forts situated strategically throughout the land.[1]

When I have a group of students with me, I will stop the bus and ask them to examine their maps in order to tell me why Teggart chose to build a fort in this particular place rather than elsewhere along the highway. A good place is Latrun on the main highway (often called the "Burma Road") between Tel Aviv and Jerusalem. Teggart's advisors were keen strategists who studied geography and history. They knew the mountains and valleys, and they understood which routes had to be controlled, which highways protected if the British were to be successful administrators of this region in the 1930s and 1940s.

Once we see the strategic importance of the landscape, I then ask if this route was important in antiquity. Did the ancient Israelites and Philistines fortify this area as well? Nine times out of ten, nearby we will discover a crusader fort and an archaeological tell, a mound that looks like a man-made hill which hides the remains of some ancient fortress or city. The conclusion is clear: ancient conquerors, just like Teggart, knew which valleys and passes had to be fortified. Strategic considerations have never changed in Israel. King David, King Herod, Titus, the Crusaders, Saladin, the Ottoman Turks, General Teggart, King Abdullah of Jordan, and Moshe Dayan of Israel all were concerned about the same valleys. While long-range artillery and air power may have changed the equation somewhat, the struggle for control of the central hills of Israel will never change.

MAJOR FEATURES OF THE LAND

Most political conflicts have a great deal to do with geography. The location of mountains, valleys, highways, bodies of water, and rainfall for agriculture all define the problem. For example, the Black Sea just north of Istanbul, Turkey, held vital warm-water ports for the Soviet Union's naval fleet. Now with the breakup of the U.S.S.R., will the Ukraine inherit these advantages—along with this massive naval fleet? These are geographical questions that have a direct bearing on a country's sense of well-being.

It is impossible to understand the complex problems of Israel/Palestine without at least a cursory knowledge of the land itself. Look carefully at the map on page 31. Israel is a small country approximately the size of the state of Vermont. For the sake of convenience, we will discuss the major regions of Israel by dividing the country north-to-south into four zones.

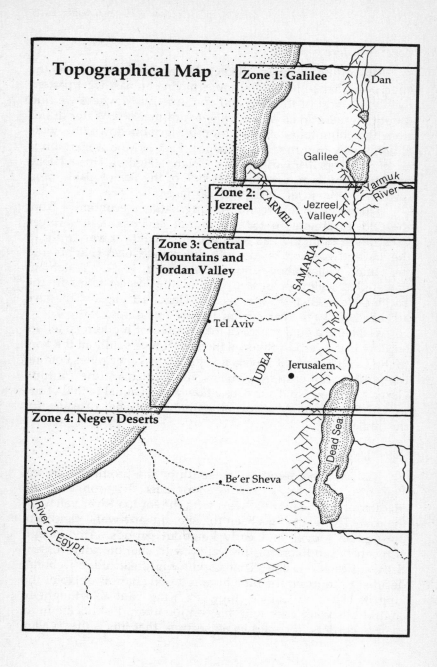

Topographical Map

Zone 1: Galilee

• Dan

Galilee

CARMEL

Yarmuk River

Zone 2: Jezreel

Jezreel Valley

Zone 3: Central Mountains and Jordan Valley

SAMARIA

• Tel Aviv

JUDEA

Jerusalem •

Zone 4: Negev Deserts

Dead Sea

• Be'er Sheva

River of Egypt

Zone 1: Galilee

The northern area is called Galilee and is dominated by the large pear-shaped lake. Mountains having an east-west pattern rise to the west of the lake and continue north where we find Mount Hermon in all of its 3,900 feet of majesty. Water drains from the mountains around Mount Hermon down the wide Huleh Valley into the Sea of Galilee. East of Mount Hermon is an elevated plateau called the Golan Heights. This plateau continues south around the east side of the Sea of Galilee and towers over it from 2,500 to 3000 feet.

The value of this region for any nation's economy—from the Old Testament to today—cannot be missed. It receives generous rainfall and has good soil. Overland caravan traffic in the ancient world traveled south down the Golan Heights into the Huleh Valley above the Sea of Galilee. In Old Testament times, this valley possessed one of the largest cities in the ancient Near East, Hazor. Today Hazor displays a massive archaeological tell that covers twenty-five acres.

Galilee is a vital source of fresh water for modern Israel. Its outflow is the Jordan River, which continues south all the way to the Dead Sea. As it travels it is joined by other rivers coming from the great eastern plateaus. In particular, the Yarmuk Gorge has a river that supplies a flow almost equal to that of the Jordan. The Yarmuk is also an essential supplier of water for the region.

Zone 2: Jezreel

Galilee is bordered on the south by the prominent Jezreel Valley. It is a break in the mountains that connects the Mediterranean Sea on the west with the Jordan River valley on the east. This valley has been the site of many wars, especially during the Judges and early kingdom periods. Any foreign army that could control this valley with chariots could essentially cut Israel in half. That is why the great judge Deborah decided to confront the nine hundred iron chariots of Jabin, the king of Hazor in Galilee (Judg. 4). King Saul also fought to control this place and, with his son Jonathan, lost his life in its eastern borders. It comes as no surprise that this is the "Valley of Armageddon." Megiddo is a fortress in the mountains of the southwest portion of the valley. "Har" means "mountains of." This is the valley beneath the "mountains of Megiddo" that will witness, according to Revelation 16:16, the final conflict of human history.

The valley has also proven to be an asset agriculturally. Generous rainfall can enter the region from the Mediterranean Sea and give it a fertility that is unsurpassed elsewhere in the country. Today the Jezreel is cultivated intensely by the Israelis.

Zone 3: The Central Mountains and Jordan Valley

From the Jezreel Valley to the southern end of the Dead Sea the land follows a consistent pattern. A central mountain range follows the Jezreel Valley diagonally (northwest to southeast), turns south when it nears the Jordan River, and then continues south for many miles. It rises to about 2,500 feet around Jerusalem and 3000 feet around Shechem and Hebron. Its western flank is made up of low rolling hills (called the Shephelah) that decrease until they become a plain near the Mediterranean Sea. This side of the mountains is extremely fertile since it catches the moist western rainfall from the sea. Thus the west is a good agricultural region. The climate has also made it a much sought-after region: witness the conflicts between the Philistines (who controlled much of the Shephelah and the coast) and the Israelites in the central mountains.

The eastern flank of the central mountains drops quickly into the Jordan Valley. These descending hills are desert because they are in a rain shadow from the central mountains. Average rainfall here is 5 to 10 inches per year while in the western Shephelah rainfall is 20 to 25 inches per year. This is often called "the Judean desert," which begins just over the hill from Bethel, Jerusalem, Bethlehem, and Hebron. The site of Jesus' wilderness temptation, these parched hills provide a formidable obstacle for anyone entering the land from the east. When Joshua entered the land this way he had to climb more than 3,700 feet in as few as 15 miles since he began at Jericho (well below sea level). When the Roman conqueror Pompey attacked Israel in 63 B.C., he came through this "back door" since it was the least expected approach.

The Jordan Valley is one of nature's miracles. It is the lowest place on the earth. The Jordan River which flows south out of Galilee culminates in the Dead Sea (about 1,275 feet below sea level). While the Jordan River is picturesque up near Galilee, in the south it winds through dreadful deserted badlands where summer temperatures regularly exceed 100 degrees. Winter is almost the only time to appreciate this region. Herod the Great built a "winter palace" for himself near Jericho to escape the winter winds in Jerusalem. Although few tourists visit it, today his pools and villas can still be seen.

East of the Jordan Valley are the mountains of Moab and Edom. The valley climbs dramatically up almost 4000 feet until it levels off on a high desert plateau. Today these mountains are in the country of Jordan. This plateau was the location of biblical Edom, Moab, and Gilead (south to north) and contained a desert highway used by Moses and the Israelites as they finished their forty-year wanderings and moved toward the Promised Land. The plateau is broken by a number of gorges that bring water down from the mountains to the Jordan Valley below.

Zone 4: The Negev Deserts

The central mountains descend and fan out into the deserts in the southernmost reaches of the country. The high Jordanian Plateau still follows the eastern border; the Jordan Valley (now waterless) is still a rift that continues beyond the Dead Sea; and in the west, deserts (called "the Negev") have populations that must live near natural springs. Isaac, for instance, decided to live in Be'er Sheva (Beersheba), which in Hebrew means "seven springs." Modern Israeli settlements here prosper only with great effort.

SUMMARY

This brief tour of the land makes it very evident that the land of Israel/Palestine has dramatic differences in quality. Life in Galilee cannot be compared with life in the Negev. Farming in Israel's western hills (the Shephelah) is good. An identical farm in the Jordan Valley must use completely different techniques.

It is interesting to study the settlement patterns of the twelve Israelite tribes with geography in mind. Benjamin (the last son of Rachel) fortunately gained the central hill country and the hills and valleys west. Judah and Ephraim and Manasseh (all privileged tribes) gained the rest of the central mountains. Dan, on the other hand, lived so far down in the Shephelah that conflict with the Philistines no doubt made the Danites migrate north to Galilee (Judg. 18). Reuben, the firstborn son of Jacob, who should have inherited the best land, settled in the high deserts on the other side of the Dead Sea. Jacob's last words to his sons in Genesis 48 and 49 describe their fate and give insight into the future life of their people.

The modern significance of this is that good land is so precious to Middle Easterners that it is passed down from generation to generation. Even the ancient Israelite Jubilee year returned lost land to families again. Today Arabs name their land—as well as every significant feature it holds (such as caves and trees and springs). Land is a treasure. And so when someone is forcibly moved from his land, or when someone says "you get 50 percent" of the land, it is important to note which 50 percent we are talking about. For this reason, Westerners miss the subtleties of many Israeli/Palestinian debates.

A BRIEF SURVEY OF OCCUPATION AND CONQUEST

One of the most difficult things to understand about Israel/Palestine is its history of conquest and occupation. Most books give more detail than we need. And modern descriptions assume we know, for instance, why the Palestinians are angry about land "taken" by Israel in 1967. Where do the British fit in? And what about these "wars" whose dates writers often parade out (1948, 1967, etc.). At the risk of oversimplifying, I shall attempt a concise summary of the last four thousand years, beginning with the tribes of Abraham and concluding with the modern era.[2] Many of the earlier dates are debated. This outline is designed for reference and comparison.

Tribal Period (2000–1000 B.C.)

In the earliest period, Abraham's tribe migrated from Mesopotamia (Iraq) into the land. Israel/Palestine was an Egyptian province called Canaan. The descendants of Abraham (Israel's twelve tribes) migrated to Egypt and remained there for more than four hundred years. Moses led them back to Canaan, and Joshua led their conquest of the land. They were loosely organized around God's tabernacle in the central mountains. However, Israel yearned to have a king and a kingdom like other nations. Saul was the first king. This was Israel's first overture to self-conscious nationhood.

The Kingdom of Israel (1000–538? B.C.)

Saul, David, and Solomon gave Israel international status, but this era of successful nationhood lasted only about seventy-five years. A civil war following the death of Solomon divided the land north and south. The north (Samaria; capital: Samaria) was conquered by the Assyrians in 721 B.C. The south (Judah; capital: Jerusalem) was conquered by Babylon in 586 B.C. Survivors from the south remained in Babylon in exile until they were freed by the Persians about fifty years later.

The Persian Period (538?–332 B.C.)

The Persian defeat of Babylon sent the Israelites home, but they were not permitted to rebuild a completely autonomous nation. Israel/Palestine was a Persian province ruled from Samaria. Jerusalem was rebuilt (Ezra, Nehemiah), and the Jews lived under Persian domination for two hundred years.

The Greek Period (332–164 B.C.)

Alexander the Great conquered the Middle East after he defeated the Persians in 333 B.C. and ⁻ ᵌde the entire region a part of the Greek Empire. For 15(ᵧears Judaism lived as a vassal under Greek rulers and adopted much of Greek culture.

The Jewish Hasmonean Kingdom (164–163 B.C.)

Jewish armies defeated their Greek overlords and established the first Jewish "kingdom" since the monarchy of the Old

Testament. However, following its victory the leadership quickly fell to corruption and internal conflict with warring factions (Pharisees and Sadducees) paralyzing the government. Many Jews dissented and departed, forming enclaves of worship in the desert (such as the Dead Sea community at Qumran).

The Roman Empire (63 B.C.–A.D. 395)

The Romans conquered the entire Middle East in the century before the birth of Christ and made it one of its provinces for more than four hundred years. The Jews were given some autonomy, but persecution was common and revolts against Rome frequent. In A.D. 66–70 Rome suppressed a major revolt and utterly destroyed Jerusalem. In A.D. 132–135 a second revolt was likewise defeated, and the Jews were expelled from Jerusalem permanently. Jewish leadership migrated to Galilee. Countless other Jews found themselves forming communities throughout Europe, North Africa, and the Middle East.

The Christian Roman Empire (A.D. 395–638)

From A.D. 395 to 638 Israel/Palestine was controlled by rulers in Constantinople (today called Istanbul, Turkey). This civilization (called Byzantine) was the grandchild of the Roman Empire and embraced Christianity as a national religion. Jerusalem witnessed the construction of many of its most famous churches in these centuries.

The Islamic Period (A.D. 638–1099)

Arabs from present-day Saudi Arabia swept north bearing the religion of Mohammed (Islam) with evangelistic zeal. All "Byzantine" provinces in the Middle East were put under siege. In 636 a major Byzantine army lost in battle at the Yarmuk River gorge, and two years later (638) Jerusalem surrendered to the Arabs. Islamic control continued until 1099. Impressive architectural remains (such as the famous "Dome of the Rock") originated in this era.

The Crusaders: Turbulence (A.D. 1099–1187)

Christian knights from Europe traveled to Israel/Palestine and recaptured the city of Jerusalem in 1099, killing all the city's residents, Jew and Muslim alike. Their control was brief, however. The Arab leader Saladin defeated the Crusaders in Galilee in 1187. The Europeans barely held a few remaining fortresses (such as Acco in the western Jezreel Valley) with the help of reinforcements from France and Britain. In 1291 they were utterly driven out (the remaining armies fleeing to Cyprus).

The Egyptian Mamlukes (A.D. 1187–1517)

For more than three hundred years, Israel/Palestine was a defensive province for an Egyptian Islamic empire that needed to guard its northern frontier. The land and its people were neglected terribly.

The Ottoman Turks (A.D. 1517–1918)

In 1517 a rival Islamic power in Istanbul, Turkey, defeated the Mamlukes and took Israel/Palestine into its realm. Ottoman control lasted four hundred years, giving the old city of Jerusalem its distinctive character we see today. For instance, the ancient walls of the city were built by the Ottoman ruler Suliman the Magnificent from 1537 to 1540.

The British Mandate (A.D. 1918–48)

Because the Turks had sided with Germany in World War I, the victors dismembered the Ottoman Empire and took the spoils. France and Britain divided up the Middle East and created most of the borders we know today. Britain initiated its control over "Palestine" (they termed it) and Jordan (as well as other areas). In 1922 they ceded control of modern-day Jordan to King Abdullah, creating the nation we know today. This arrangement continued through World War II. But with the increase of Jewish immigration from Europe, conflicts with the Palestinian Arabs, and Britain's exhaustion following the war, the British lost their desire to remain in the land. In 1947 the United Nations proposed a partition of Palestine in order to make an Arab and a Jewish state.[3] Despite extreme Arab resentment, Israel raised its new flag with the star of David on May 14, 1948. Within minutes President Truman of the United States gave it formal recognition. At once the Arabs declared war.

The First War: 1948, "The War of Independence"

Known as Israel's war of independence, Israeli and Arab armies fought viciously to change the boundries. King Abdullah of Jordan no doubt had dreams of taking everything, including land promised to Israel. Other Arabs were offended even by the notion of an Israeli state. Israel won decisively and redrew the map, acquiring more land than was offered in the United Nations Partition. At the close of the war, Israel occupied 77 percent of the land (33 percent more than the U.N. proposal). Nevertheless, Jordan occupied the West Bank of the Jordan River (all the way into the central mountains, including the cities of Nablus, Ramallah, and Hebron). Jordan also possessed the eastern half of the city of Jerusalem. Even though the Partition Plan of 1947 anticipated a Palestinian state, Jordan later annexed the West Bank (issuing Jordanian citizenship papers and passports there). In the end, hopes for a Palestinian state free of Israeli and Jordanian rule evaporated overnight.

The Second War: 1956, "The Sinai War"

Hostilities continued for eight years, generally in the form of guerrilla attacks. Since 1948 Egypt had closed the Suez Canal to Israeli shipping. In 1955 Egypt was strengthened by generous Soviet military aid and blockaded the Gulf of Aqaba/Eilat. Israel attacked Egypt (with French assistance) in October 1956, captured the entire Sinai Desert, and threatened to attack Cairo. With pressure from America, Israel withdrew so long as Egypt would maintain a peaceful border and not interfere with Israeli shipping.

The Third War: 1967, "The Six-Day War"

Border conflicts continued for eleven years with Syria, Jordan, and Egypt. By 1966 it was clear that all of the countries were bracing for war.[4] Egypt called it "a holy war" to defeat the

Jews. Heavy-armor divisions began forming on all of Israel's borders. In June of 1967 Israel struck first by launching an air strike that virtually wiped out the Egyptian air force on the ground.[5] By nightfall, Israel destroyed 416 Arab planes. In less than a week, it was over. Israel had won decisively. Israel expanded its borders again, occupying the entire West Bank (to the Jordan River), the Golan Heights, the Sinai, and the entire city of Jerusalem. Previously Israel had 8,500 square miles. Now it added another 2,800 square miles, an increase of 33 percent.

The Fourth War: 1973, "The Yom Kippur War"

On October 6, 1973—the Jewish holy day of Yom Kippur—Egyptian and Syrian armies surprised Israel with a land invasion of the Sinai and the Golan Heights in an attempt to regain lost land. The assault, while not long-lived, sobered the Israelis considerably. The Soviet Union had supplied the Arabs with excellent technology that could match the American weapons held in Israel.[6] Israel counterattacked, drove back the Arab forces, and crossed the Suez Canal. Under United Nations cease-fire and disengagement agreements, Israel withdrew from the canal's west bank and later yielded the Sinai oil fields.

In this less tense atmosphere, Anwar Sadat made a surprise visit to Menachem Begin in 1977, paving the way for a meeting at Camp David in 1979. The accords reached at the meeting included a formal peace treaty, establishing of diplomatic relations, and Israel's complete withdrawal from the Sinai. They also stipulated that this peace "be linked" to full autonomy for the Palestinians. Sadat's courageous overture cost him his life, as he was killed by Egyptian radicals opposed to the peace process.

The Fifth War: 1982, "The Invasion of Lebanon"

In June Israel invaded Lebanon in an attempt to destroy the Palestinian forces that used southern Lebanon to launch attacks against Israel. Israeli tanks rolled all the way to the edge of Beirut, and their artillery shelled the city, indiscriminately killing thousands and thousands of Lebanese citizens. The following year Israel began to withdraw under U.N. pressure and objections from its own citizens ("Israel's Vietnam," they called it), but Israel kept a buffer zone in southern Lebanon. Complete withdrawal from Lebanon came in 1985. However, in 1981 Israel annexed the Golan Heights, making it a formal part of the country.[7]

The Sixth War: 1987, "The Unofficial War, The Intifada"

During each of the previous wars, the Palestinians residing in and around Israel were becoming the pawns in a larger Middle Eastern poker game. Tensions in the West Bank and Gaza finally erupted in 1987. Legend credits a vehicle accident in Gaza for the start of the Intifada, in which Palestinian civilians began using civil disobedience (throwing stones, etc.) to thwart Israeli control and inspire international sympathy. Palestinian stones confronted Israeli Uzzi submachine guns on television networks worldwide. Intifada does not mean "uprising." Palestinians say it means "to shake off aggressively as if a scorpion had suddenly appeared on your arm."[8] The Intifada continues today as a popular movement of economic and political resistance supported by a broad spectrum of Palestinians. It is a war unlike any other the region has ever witnessed. And for Israel, it may be the most threatening. In 1991 the Intifada began to lose momentum, especially as Russian immigrants arrived in Israel and the country had less need of cheap Arab labor. Today street conflicts are rare except in the Gaza Strip.

Refugees

Most of these major military conflicts produced refugees who fled their homes because of the war and then were refused permission to return. According to the United Nations, in 1987 there were 2,201,123 Palestinian refugees. Of these 373,000 live in the West Bank and 445,000 live in Gaza. The West Bank now has twenty refugee camps, Gaza has eight, Lebanon has twelve, and Jordan and Syria each have ten.[9] What is surprising is how these refugees still remember their villages and their histories. In the large camp of Jalazone outside Ramallah, a family once explained their history to me in detail. Their home once had been under the runways of Tel Aviv's Ben Gurion International Airport. In 1948 they were driven out by the

army. Some extent of the disaster to Palestinian villages can be
seen in the following statistics: of about 807 registered Palestinian villages in 1945, only 433 were still standing by 1967. Put
bluntly, 45 percent of the Palestinian villages were emptied and
demolished as a result of the creation of the state of Israel.[10] As
Israel acquired land, one of its specific goals was to depopulate
the areas acquired. The Palestinians fell victim to propaganda
campaigns telling them to flee. Many Arab countries affirmed
the wisdom of flight on the assumption that everyone could
return home.

One of my neighbors spent most of his life in a kibbutz
near Gaza during those turbulent years. He tells how in 1948
Israeli planes dropped leaflets in the Palestinian villages
warning the people to get out or else they would all be killed.
After they left, Israeli settlers simply moved into the Palestinian
homes. Some of the villages were destroyed by dynamite, and
some were plowed under for agricultural areas. Others are now
buried in reforestation projects.

THE MODERN EQUATION

Both the land of Israel and history of its occupation must
be understood in order for us to have some grasp of the nature
of the modern conflict. This has led to a remarkably tense
situation in which Israel struggles for international credibility,
Israel's neighbors have grievances based on war and loss of
land, and over two million Palestinian refugees seek their home
in the midst of the conflict.

Further, Arabs grieve the loss of control in this land where
Islamic empires have had the upper hand for 1,200 of the last
2,000 years. The success of Israel—militarily as well as economically—has shamed Arab pride significantly. This is one reason
the Arab world is pleased to see Western dependence on its oil.
Since the 1970s, oil has reaped considerable political leverage
for the Arab world.

The map on page 43 shows the political boundaries that
define the modern debates about Israel/Palestine. Israel is a
remarkably small country. It is about 40 miles from the western
Mediterranean coast to the Jordan River in the east. It is about

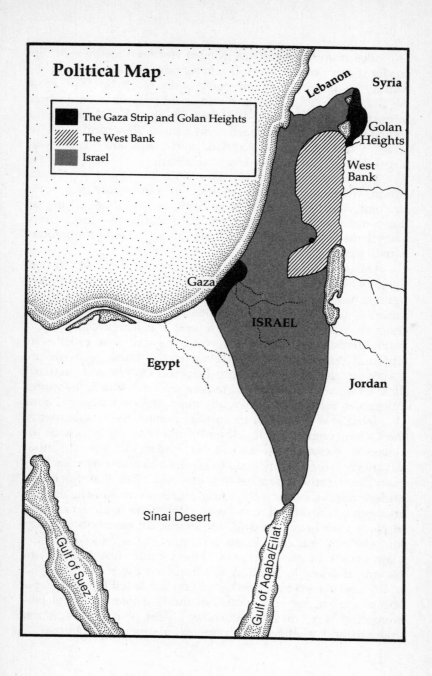

Political Map

⬛	The Gaza Strip and Golan Heights
▨	The West Bank
▦	Israel

Lebanon

Syria

Golan
Heights

West
Bank

Gaza

ISRAEL

Egypt

Jordan

Sinai Desert

Gulf of Suez

Gulf of Aqaba/Eilat

140 miles from the far north (Mount Hermon) to the southern border (Be'er Sheva). From the mountains in the center of the country, a good artillery unit could easily reach Tel Aviv. From the Golan Heights, a mortar round could land almost anywhere in northern Galilee. An F-16 fighter flying out of Amman, the capital of Jordan, could reach Jerusalem in 75 seconds and Tel Aviv in three minutes.[11] Syrians and Iraqis alike can easily target Israel with unsophisticated missiles.

This close proximity explains the entire region's preoccupation with security. Every piece of real estate has some strategic value. So when people begin to talk about slicing up the country to build, say, a parallel Palestinian state, almost every Israeli shudders to think how this might alter the military equation.

Lebanon borders Israel in the north above Galilee. It is in the low, rolling hills of southern Lebanon that Palestinian fighters have historically built bases to reenter and attack Israel. Lebanon is perceived by Israel as an unstable region and a serious area of vulnerability. In 1982 the Israelis launched a major attack into Lebanon, sweeping the area clean of Palestinians and carrying their fight even to the outskirts of Beirut. Today Israel watches southern Lebanon closely and regularly flies its jets there on reconnaissance and attack missions. Palestinian refugees are currently migrating back into this area.

Syria is at the northeast corner of Israel. Syria once owned the Golan Heights but lost them in the war of 1967. Since the Golan is elevated (to almost 3000 feet), it has a serious advantage over the lowlands of Galilee. So many mortars have been fired on the kibbutzes of northern Galilee that most have underground shelters today. Above ground the Israelis devised an ingenious means of protection: loose stone boulders are held in place with heavy fencing, forming small twenty-by-twenty-foot shelters that can absorb the impact of a direct hit. After many years of these attacks, Israel could not tolerate the security risk any longer and so conquered the plateau in 1967. In 1973 Syria tried to regain the region but failed in the midst of one of the largest tank battles of modern history. Israel later annexed this region in 1981. Today Galilee is quiet. Traditional underground shelters are popular places for kibbutzes to sponsor dances. The bomb-proof walls are likewise rock music proof.

The Golan Heights is an eerie no-man's land. An abandoned Syrian city called Quneitra sits on the plateau like a ghost town. The flank of Mount Hermon nearby bristles with high-tech surveillance devices that keep an eye on everything that moves. Today the United Nations maintains a buffer zone between the two armies. (The soldiers from other countries always seem to arouse the curiosity of tourists who visit the fence border.)

Jordan shares a long border with Israel from south of the Sea of Galilee (along the Yarmuk River gorge), along the Jordan River itself, to the gulf of Aqaba in the south. Hot springs on the Yarmuk River date back to Roman times (Hammet Gader). Visitors who like adventure can sit in the hot springs and then climb the hill to watch Israeli guards and Jordanian soldiers staring at each other with high-powered binoculars.

From 1948 until the war of 1967, the Jordanian border used to cross over the Jordan River and extend into the central mountains, encompassing the Arab cities of Nablus (biblical Shechem), Ramallah, Bethlehem, and Hebron. In fact, just north of Jerusalem (in the village of Shuafat) are a curious little airport and palace that were being built by King Hussein of Jordan before he lost the mountains to Israel. Today they still stand incomplete. The land from the Jordan River into the mountains is traditionally called "the West Bank," referring to the west side of the Jordan River.

In the war of 1967 Jordan lost the West Bank to Israel. From a strategic standpoint this was a significant achievement for Israel. Today Israel occupies all of the highlands inside the country and uses the deep gorge of the Jordan River as a natural barrier against attacks from the east. High-tech sensors and electric fences stretch along this eastern frontier. Near the Israeli highway that skirts the border, a double fence is separated by soft sand that is combed daily by an army patrol looking for the footprints of intruders.

In the far south are the great deserts that extend from the region south of the Dead Sea all the way west to the Mediterranean. As we noted above, these deserts are a buffer between Israel and Egypt. Israel conquered them in 1956, returned them, reconquered them in 1967, nearly lost them in 1973, and then as a result of a 1979 treaty returned them again in 1982.

THE CENTRAL ISSUE: TAKING LAND

The pattern is evident. Israel has a considerable security problem. Israel is surrounded by hostile armies because Israel occupies land that is hotly disputed by most of its neighbors.

In each of the major wars, Israel strategically increased the size of its holdings at the expense of Lebanon, Egypt, Syria, and Jordan. Consider the following statistics gleaned from the records of the United Nations: When the United Nations General Assembly approved a plan to divide the country into an Israeli state and a Palestinian state on November 29, 1947, the breakdown of land and population looked like this:

	Arabs (Muslims and Christians)	Jews
% of Population	69	31
% of Land Owned or Settled	94	6
% Land Offered in U.N. Plan	48	52

At once the relative inequity is evident: 31 percent of the population living on 6 percent of the land was being given half the country! Let us look at one district (as the British organized the area) and see how this worked out. In Nazareth District in 1945, the Arab population was 84 percent and the Jewish population was 16 percent. Land ownership broke down thus: Arab: 52 percent, Jewish: 28 percent, public lands: 20 percent. Therefore it made sense to give this region to the Palestinians. But consider the neighboring Galilee District. Arab population: 67 percent, Jewish population: 33 percent. Land holdings: Arab: 51 percent, Jewish: 38 percent, public lands: 11 percent. Yet this area near the Sea of Galilee was given to Israel.[12]

When Israel declared itself a state on May 14, 1948, the Arabs took offense that Westerners would divide their land and then offer them such a slice! King Abdullah of Jordan no doubt saw this as an attempt to limit his growing control. At the close of the war, Israel even exceeded its allotted holdings significantly: instead of possessing 52 percent of the land as the United Nations urged, Israel held 77 percent of it. This is one-third more than the original U.N. plan.

The next major territorial increase came in the spring of 1967. Within a week, Israel captured the entire Sinai desert, the "West Bank" including east Jerusalem, Gaza, and the Golan Heights. This was a watershed event, for in one campaign, Israel virtually doubled its size by taking huge chunks of Syria, Jordan, and Egypt.

These lands are called today "the Occupied Territories" in the political jargon of the Middle East. And they are sorely disputed. On November 22, 1967, the United Nations passed Resolution 242 (perhaps the most famous resolution for Israel and the Palestinians), declaring that Israel must withdraw from these territories. The United States agreed to the resolution, and ever since then Resolution 242 has played a pivotal role in all discussions. Even though Israel returned the Sinai to Egypt in 1982, Israel still holds the Golan Heights (annexed in December 1981), Gaza, and the West Bank, along with their Palestinian populations. Today Israel has even annexed East Jerusalem.

Look once more at the map. Consider the military advantages that come to anyone holding the mountains (the West Bank) and the Golan Heights above Galilee. Consider the religious and psychological importance of capturing Jerusalem in its entirety and making it a new capital. Israeli strategists, like Joshua long ago, know precisely what they are doing.

ANCIENT AND MODERN TIMES COMPARED

The story I have just summarized is nothing new to the Middle East. Since the earliest days when Joshua surveyed this land with his lieutenants, every leader has been forced to consider how to control this narrow strip of real estate. Four facts must be kept in mind:

1. Israel/Palestine is an ancient highway. Thousands of years ago the superpowers of the ancient world were Egypt in the south and the kingdoms of Mesopotamia in the north (particularly Assyria and Babylon, today in modern Iraq). Because the deserts of Arabia and Syria do not permit easy passage, caravans (in peacetime) and armies (in war) traveled along a coastal route between the desert and the sea, directly through Israel/Palestine. They would hug the coast, traveling between the hills and the coastal swamps, finding easy passage to their destinations. Keep in mind that Abraham and Sarah were from Iraq. When God called them to travel south, they followed this ancient highway.

This means that even today, Israel/Palestine plays a pivotal geographical role. Travel from Turkey or Syria or Lebanon to Egypt must pass through Israel/Palestine if it is going to avoid a major detour. Some strategists in Washington see the American alliance with Israel as serving a similar modern purpose. Israel is an outpost, a Western friend, a point of access to the larger Middle East.

2. Life in Israel/Palestine is dangerous. In peacetime long ago the coastal regions offered access to the great trade route, but in war, armies moving north and south laid waste to every city and fortress in the region. Abraham must have known this when he climbed into these mountains and settled there, leaving the ancient highway behind. In later years Israel became a mountain kingdom, extending west through the hills and into the coast only when it was safe (see the stories of Samson and the Philistines and of Eli and his sons as examples). This is why Jerusalem (the capital of King David) is tucked away high in the mountains—as is Samaria, the capital of the breakaway northern kingdom in the Old Testament. These were good places to build defenses against marauding foreigners.

Is it any surprise that Israel refuses to give up the West Bank? It is hardly just the west bank of the Jordan River! The West Bank is really the highlands, the mountains from Nablus to Hebron called "Samaria and Judea" by Israeli leaders. These mountains provide refuge and safety. In war they offer the possessor an astonishing advantage. Foreign armies from distant places—such as Greece and Rome in the ancient world, the Crusaders in medieval times, and the British this century— have learned the awesome advantage of these mountains the hard way.

3. *Life in Israel/Palestine is precarious.* Perhaps the most precious commodity in Israel is water. When Moses described the land to the Israelites, this was one of the first items he wanted to clarify: "For the land that you are about to enter to occupy is not like the land of Egypt, from which you have come, where you sow your seed and irrigate by foot like a vegetable garden" (Deut. 11:10). In the next verses, Moses goes on to tell the people that rainfall is one tool that God uses in this land to bless or to discipline the people. Why is this a problem? The Jordan River is in a deep gorge almost 4000 feet below the central mountains. The Sea of Galilee has abundant water, but only this century has the Israeli government effectively pumped its water throughout the country by pipe. In the winter of 1991–92 record snow and rain fell, bringing up the water levels, and the entire nation celebrated!

This means that Israel struggles for some of its natural resources. The land is a hard land that requires the people who would subdue it to have faith in God. Every century the use of these limited resources must be negotiated carefully with Israel's neighbors. Today, considering the value of Galilee's water, what does it mean if Jordan has lost access to it? What does it mean when Palestinian villagers are not permitted to dig new wells while neighboring Jewish settlements have sprinkler systems for their lawns with piped-in Galilee water? Within Israel, hundreds and hundreds of Palestinian villages have been destroyed by bulldozers because they sat on excellent land. Today careful observers can identify these silent villages because the cactuses (the Sabra) used by the Arabs for fencing continue to grow back.

4. *"When the cat's away the mice will play."* In the absence of dominating superpowers (ancient Egypt, Assyria, Babylon, Greece, Rome—or today, Turkey and Britain), the regional nations struggle for dominance. In the Old Testament the

Israelites fought against the Philistines (on the coast), the Edomites and the Moabites (in modern-day Jordan), the Ammonites (in modern Syria), and the Phoenicians (in modern Lebanon). Each country leveraged its power against others. Unusual treaties were formed—such as Ahab's alliance with Phoenicia.

This pattern of regional struggle is no different today. The desert kingdom of Jordan has precious few resources and historically has always laid claim to lands west of the Jordan River. For example, Amman, the capital of Jordan, gets less than half the rainfall that Jerusalem does. Syria likewise values the good agricultural potential of the Golan Heights and Lebanon. In New Testament times the Golan (called Gaulinitis and Batanea) was used for grain production by the Romans because it gets sufficient rain each year for a cereal crop.

SUMMARY

In order to win at Monopoly, we have to know the playing board. In order to understand the life and death game being played in Israel/Palestine, we have to understand the major geographical issues that have been weighed for thousands of years. Who will occupy the best land in this country? Where will they live? Can they defend themselves?

The struggle for this land is not new. Its contours have been known from earliest times. When Alexander the Great conquered the land in 332 B.C., he wisely built his regional administrative center in Samaria. He knew the advantages. The remains of his buildings can be seen today just west of modern Nablus. When General Teggart surveyed the land for the British in 1937, legend has it that he studied the Bible, especially the book of Joshua. From these notes and the input of his Middle Eastern advisors, he planned the British occupation of Israel/Palestine. Ancient principles are still at work.

NOTES

    1. Robert John and Sami Hadawi, *The Palestine Diary*, 2 vols. (New York: New World Press, 1970), 1:280; Menachem Begin, *The Revolt* (Los Angeles: Nash, 1948), 91.

2. For a more complete history penned by evangelical writers, see W. G. Pippert, *Land of Promise, Land of Strife. Israel at Forty* (Waco: Word, 1988), 42–76; S. A. Ellisen, *The Arab-Israeli Conflict. Who Owns the Land?* (Portland: Multnomah, 1991), 37–166; and especially P. Johnson, *A History of the Jews* (New York: Harper & Row, 1987). Secular histories are in abundance. C. Roth, *A History of the Jews* (New York: Schocken Books, 1961, 1970).

3. A detailed map showing the borders of the partition is difficult to find. An excellent scholarly edition can be found in H. Cattan, *Palestine, the Arabs and Israel. The Search for Justice* (London: Longman, 1969), 207. Generally, the land was to be partitioned in three sections: 4,500 square miles for the Jewish state, and Jerusalem to be set off as an international island for both parties and all religions.

4. The Arabs were poised to field about 540,000 troops, 2,500 tanks, and 950 aircraft. The Israelis had 265,000 troops, 800 tanks, and 300 aircraft.

5. Many Christian writers still debate this contrary to academic historical studies. Note Ron Cantrell, "This territory was acquired defensively by Israel in two Arab wars of aggression against her (1967 and 1973)" *Bridges for Peace* 16, 4 (1991): 8. Nothing could be further from the truth. Historians agree that in 1967 both sides were spoiling for a fight, and Israel felt abandoned and surrounded. Israel struck first. In 1973 the Arabs struck first. Compare the article "Israel, History," in *Encyclopedia Britannica* (Macropaedia) (Chicago, 1974), 22:144. Cf. the accurate detailed description of S. A. Ellisen, *Who Owns the Land?* 112–15.

6. According to Ellisen, *Who Owns the Land?* (p. 119), the Soviets contributed $3.5 billion to the Arabs, and the United States contributed $2.2 billion to Israel.

7. For an outstanding study of the invasion of Lebanon written by a Christian pastor, see Peter Crooks, *Lebanon. The Pain and the Glory* (Eastborne, Sussex: Monarch, 1990). Formerly an Anglican chaplain in Beirut and Damascus, Crooks now lives in England. The book is enthusiastically endorsed by the Anglican bishop of Jerusalem.

8. This definition was given to me by Father Elias Chacour in his village of Ibillin, Galilee, in 1989.

9. Pippert, *Israel at Forty*, 111.

10. Sabri Jiryis, *The Arabs in Israel*, trans. from Arabic by Inea Bushnaq (New York: Monthly Review Press, 1976), 70. Lists of Palestinian villages can be found in official Israeli publications. For 1967 see *Census of Populations 1967* (Central Bureau of Statistics), *West*

Bank of the Jordan, Gaza Strip and Northern Sinai, Golan Heights.
Publication 1 (Jerusalem, 1967), 45–49, 163–65.

11. M. Widlanski, *Can Israel Survive a Palestinian State?* (Jerusalem:
Institute for Advanced Strategic and Political Studies, 1990), 32–33.

12. See the government statistics given in H. Cattan, *Palestine, the
Arabs and Israel. The Search for Justice* (London: Longman, 1969), 18–30,
207–10. This data is based on U.N. Statistics, British Administration
reports, and village land records.

Part Two

The Old Testament
and the Land

Chapter Three

PROMISES OF LAND

"On that day the LORD made a covenant with Abram,
saying, 'To your descendants I give this land, from the river
of Egypt to the great river, the river Euphrates, the land of
the Kenites, the Kenizzites, the Kadmonites, the Hittites,
the Perizzites, the Rephaim, the Amorites, the Canaanites,
the Girgashites, and the Jebusites.' " (Gen. 15:18–21)

"The land shall not be sold in perpetuity, for the land is
mine; with me you are but aliens and tenants. Throughout
the land that you hold, you shall provide for the redemption
of the land." (Lev. 25:23–24)

The ancient walled city of Jerusalem is divided into four
quarters. For centuries this tradition has been respected, giving
the city its distinctive character. The Jewish Quarter (southeast), the Armenian Quarter (southwest), the Christian Quarter
(northwest), and the Muslim Quarter (northeast) all preserve
ancient communities that venerate unique holy sites.[1] The
Christian Quarter, for example, consists of about forty-five
acres and is centered on the magnificent Church of the Holy
Sepulchre, the traditional place of Jesus' crucifixion and burial.
Christians from all over the world pilgrimage to this place and
there can witness worship in progress as Latin and Eastern
traditions celebrate mass and Protestant charismatics sing and
pray in chapels carved into the stone walls.

In early 1990 a group of Israeli settlers broke with tradition. Carefully disguising their plan, they purchased St. John's Hospice in the Christian Quarter under false pretenses and began to move in—a move that offended even Jerusalem's mayor, Teddy Kollek, who respects the privileges of each faith community in the city. The hospice, which stands between the Greek Convent of St. John and the sacred Church of the Holy Sepulchre, has been owned for centuries by the Greek Orthodox Church, and in the Old City of Jerusalem, *no one sells property like this.*

During Holy Week, on Maunday Thursday, 150 Jewish settlers moved in protected by the army. When the traditional Orthodox Holy Week procession came through the city, they stopped at St. John's and tried to remove Israel's flags, which covered sacred Christian symbols. The entire crowd was teargassed.

Protests erupted everywhere. The Church of the Holy Sepulchre was closed down on Easter for the first time in history. Christians throughout the Middle East—Protestant, Catholic, and Orthodox—saw this as an unprecedented offense.[2] In fact, when the Greek patriarch Diodoros and many of his bishops came to the building in protest, these elderly dignified men were roughed up by soldiers and teargassed in front of television cameras. Bishop Timothy, the general secretary to the patriarch, commented that "it was a violation of the status quo of church property" in Jerusalem.

I happened to be in Jerusalem that spring and thought it would be interesting to see what all the fuss was about. The government had demanded that most of the settlers leave and only a "symbolic group" remain to occupy the property. As I rounded the corner, soldiers were everywhere, and I could see Hebrew graffiti that aggressively laid claim to the property. What looked like sheets covered up the Christian symbols on the building, and the "star of David" was spray-painted generously on the walls.

As I looked on at the tense scene, two teenage boys from the settlement stopped me. They were eager to explain to a tourist what this meant. And so I listened.

"We have bought what is ours anyway, and how we did it doesn't matter," they said.

I asked if it were not true that the Greeks had owned this property for hundreds of years—maybe even a thousand years.

"It doesn't matter," they answered. "God gave us this country and this city, and Jews can live anywhere."

I reflected on the fact that Greek Christians could not buy land in the Jewish Quarter.

"We are only taking what is ours by right. These people have no right even to be in this city," they replied.

This last thought enticed me. And so I pursued this idea of "rights" with these seventeen-year-old zealots.

"God gave this land to Abraham, and we are his descendants. It belongs to us. Everything that happened in between simply doesn't matter. The Palestinian Christians should just get out."

The conversation struck me as odd because these boys were American. They were from New York and had been in the country only a few years. And here they were ejecting an ancient Christian community that could trace its history to this bit of real estate for more than a thousand years. And, ironically, it was a community that likewise claimed descent from Abraham. Did God promise the land to Judaism? What do the Scriptures say? Was the promise confirmed later? Did it come with conditions?

THE ORIGINAL PROMISES

The source of this argument used by the Israeli teenagers in Jerusalem can be found in Genesis 12. When God called Abraham, he made two promises. One promise concerned Abraham's children—whose number would exceed the stars in the sky. The other concerned land since Abraham was nomadic and had no land of his own. These two items—children and land—reside at the center of Middle Eastern life even today. One promises the continuing survival of name and heritage; the other promises a place, a refuge, a locale called "home." Today an Arab man is commonly known as "the father" of his firstborn son.[3] Arab village farmers likewise esteem their land by giving personal names to its trees, its springs, and its caves. The introductory verses of the Abraham story begin with an outline of God's promise.

> Now the LORD said to Abram, "Go from your country and your kindred and your father's house to the land that I will show you. I will make of you a great nation, and I will bless you, and make your name great, so that you will be a blessing. I will bless those who bless you, and the one who curses you I will curse; and in you all the families of the earth shall be blessed." (Gen. 12:1–3)

Strikingly, this promise fails to mention the land. Virtually every scholar who studies the passage notes that this is peculiar.[4] In some sense, the primary thrust of the story is that Abraham is going to be the father of a nation, and it is their identity as God's people that is most important, not necessarily where they live. This makes sense when we consider that Abraham was nomadic, traveling between Mesopotamia (his home, Iraq) and the Egyptian province of Canaan (what we commonly call Israel/Palestine today). This original promise addressed the migratory life of the patriarch. It is a promise for new pasture for the nomad, his clan, and his animals to escape the threat of starvation.[5] As Abraham's story continues, it is interesting that Abraham does not settle down. He moves his tents among the cities of Shechem, Bethel, Hebron, and Be'er Sheva. He does not buy any land or possess any land until Sarah dies and he needs a burial site.

A brief form of this promise is mentioned in Genesis 13:14–17. After Abraham scans the countryside in all directions, God says, "The land that you see I will give to you and to your offspring forever. . . . Rise up, walk through the length and the breadth of the land, for I will give it to you."

This promise is formally reaffirmed in Genesis 15 when God makes a covenant with Abraham. In 15:1–6 the land is omitted once again, but in 15:18–21, God speaks clearly about the land inheritance that Abraham will receive.

> On that day the LORD made a covenant with Abram, saying, "To your descendants I give this land, from the river of Egypt to the great river, the river Euphrates, the land of the

Kenites, the Kenizzites, the Kadmonites, the Hittites, the Perizzites, the Rephaim, the Amorites, the Canaanites, the Girgashites, and the Jebusites." (Gen. 15:18–21)

Again in Genesis 17 when Abraham's name is changed (formerly it had been Abram) God repeats the twofold promise for progeny and land:

"I will establish my covenant between me and you, and your offspring after you throughout their generations, for an everlasting covenant, to be God to you and to your offspring after you. And I will give to you, and to your offspring after you, the land where you are now an alien, all the land of Canaan, for a perpetual holding; and I will be their God."

God said to Abraham, "As for you, you shall keep my covenant, you and your offspring after you throughout their generations." (Gen. 17:7–9)

One thing is exceedingly clear. This gift of land is intimately connected to the covenant, or contract, that God is making with Abraham. It is a "package deal" that includes the following elements:

- Abraham will receive the land as an everlasting possession;
- Abraham's posterity will become a great nation;
- An everlasting covenant will bind Abraham and his descendants to God.
- All of the people of the earth will be blessed through Abraham and his people.[6]

In order to make clear that this promise extends to Abraham's children, Genesis repeats these promises for Isaac (Abraham's son) in 26:2–4 and for Jacob (Abraham's grandson through Isaac) in 28:13–15. But in all cases—even when it is repeated elsewhere in the Old Testament—the promise to Abraham is the anchor passage. In fact, when Israel later disobeys the Lord and the prophets announce punishment, it will be God's promise to Abraham that brings hope of restoration and forgiveness (Jer. 7:7; 16:15; Ezek. 3:24; cf. Deut. 8:18). Micah 7:20 says it succinctly: "You will show faithfulness to Jacob and unswerving loyalty to Abraham, as you have sworn to our ancestors from the days of old.'"[7]

Some interpreters would have us pause here and ask us carefully to identify the recipients of these promises. If the promise is extended to Abraham's children, its reaffirmation to Isaac does not necessarily exclude the promise to Ishmael (the reputed father of the Arabs).[8] Later the Old Testament does narrow the scope of the promise, but it may not have been like this originally. Even when Ishmael and his mother Hagar are expelled, God promises that Ishmael will produce a great nation "because he is your offspring" (21:13). Indeed, Abraham's descendants will be named through Isaac (21:12), but it is unclear if the promise of land is then taken away from Ishmael. Curiously, when the covenant of circumcision is made in Genesis 17 and the land of Canaan is promised, it is Ishmael who is circumcised (Gen. 17:25–27). Isaac was not even born.

As we read the story of Abraham carefully, three things stand out. First, the native residents of this province called Canaan are not displaced. They are not ejected from their homes. Instead, Abraham becomes a neighbor (not a conqueror) who enters into trade relations with the indigenous people of the land. This cannot be stressed enough. When Sarah dies (Gen. 23), Abraham does not presume that he can simply take any burial ground he desires. He must buy it. In fact, Genesis 23 records a lengthy negotiation in which Ephron the Hittite who owns the field Abraham desires to buy tries to give the property to Abraham as a gift. Abraham refuses to accept it. He insists on buying it. Before an array of legal witnesses at Hebron's city gate, Abraham finally purchases the cave of Machpelah near the Oaks of Mamre.[9] Keep in mind that Ephron was a Hittite—one of the very people listed in Genesis 15:20 whose land Abraham was going to inherit. Yet here Abraham treats the Hittites with considerable respect.

Second, the story emphasizes that land is linked with covenant. Genesis 17:9 affirms Abraham's responsibility, and it follows right on the heels of 17:8, which contains the land promise. It is not as if a "title deed" had been handed to Abraham and God was no longer part of the picture. Rather, the land is an outgrowth of the relationship between Abraham,

Abraham's descendants, and God. In this relationship there is no doubt that the land is to be an everlasting possession, but it assumes faithfulness to a relationship with God. The law books Leviticus and Deuteronomy will later make this clear. The prophets will likewise remind Israel that this dimension cannot be ignored.

Finally, God emphasizes that Abraham's children will become "a great nation" and through them "all of the peoples of the earth will be blessed." Frequently evangelicals have taken Genesis 12:2–3 out of context:

> "I will make of you a great nation, and I will bless you, and make your name great, so that you will be a blessing. I will bless those who bless you, and the one who curses you I will curse; and in you all the families of the earth shall be blessed."

The idea here is not that the gentiles must somehow support Israelite efforts at greatness and nationhood and in so doing discover the blessing of God. Nor (in its original setting) does it mean that the blessing of the families of the earth will come about because Israel will bring the world its messiah, Jesus Christ.[10] Rather, this passage suggests that through Israel's greatness, through Israel's goodness, because Israel is blessed, God's people will in turn be able to bless and enrich the lives of others living nearby. In other words, there will be an *ethical* dimension to Israel's relation with God. The covenant is not designed simply to satisfy Israel's nationhood and give it land. Nor is the covenant designed to satisfy Israel's self-interest. The covenant with Israel is God's strategy to bring his goodness and righteousness to the rest of humanity. Israel is to be a nation of priests (Ex. 19:6; Deut. 7:6) mediating God's presence and goodness to the earth.

PROMISES WITH CONDITIONS

The connection between covenant fidelity and the promise of land is evident throughout the Torah (the five traditional books of Moses). Possessing the land was contingent on Israel's consistently living by God's righteous standards.[11] One of the most surprising discoveries for me was how rarely this theme is sounded by evangelical writers. For example, John Walvoord's *Armageddon, Oil, and the Middle East Crisis* contains a discussion of the promises of land to Israel but neglects this material completely![12]

Both Leviticus and Deuteronomy warn Israel about righteousness and the land in dramatic terms. In fact, the images are shocking! If Israel does not obey God's laws, then the land itself will vomit the nation out. Leviticus 18 and 20 were given at Mount Sinai, where God was exceedingly explicit about his covenant and its obligations. Chapter 18 warns Israel against taking on the lifestyle of the Canaanites:

> Do not defile yourselves in any of these ways, for by all these practices the nations I am casting out before you have defiled themselves. Thus the land became defiled; and I punished it for its iniquity, and the land vomited out its inhabitants. But you shall keep my statutes and my ordinances and commit none of these abominations, either the citizen or the alien who resides among you (for the inhabitants of the land, who were before you, committed all of these abominations, and the land became defiled); *otherwise the land will vomit you out for defiling it, as it vomited out the nation that was before you.* For whoever commits any of these abominations shall be cut off from their people. So keep my charge not to commit any of these abominations that were done before you, and not to defile yourselves by them: I am the LORD your God. (Lev. 18:24–30. *Emphasis mine.*)

Chapter 20 turns its attention to the expectations of ritual holiness within the covenant:

> You shall keep all my statutes and all my ordinances, and observe them, *so that the land to which I bring you to settle in may not vomit you out.* You shall not follow the practices of the nation that I am driving out before you. Because they did all these things, I abhorred them. But I have said to you: You shall inherit their land, and I will give it to you to possess, a land flowing with milk and honey. I am the LORD your God; I have separated you from the peoples. You shall therefore make a distinction between the clean animal and

the unclean, and between the unclean bird and the clean; you shall not bring abomination on yourselves by animal or by bird or by anything with which the ground teems, which I have set apart for you to hold unclean. You shall be holy to me; for I the LORD am holy, and I have separated you from the other peoples to be mine. (Lev. 20:22–26. *Emphasis mine.*)

Note how Moses emphasizes holiness. And note how in each case it is the land itself that will eject its inhabitants. This is because the land has a life of its own (as we shall see below, it is God's land) and can suffer abuse and be defiled. Unrighteousness defiles the land of Israel/Palestine. Just as grievous sinners were ejected from the camp of Israel lest further wrongdoing increase, so too, Israel could be ejected from the camp or land of God.

After the wilderness wanderings, Moses led the people across the south end of the Dead Sea, up onto the plateau that is today Jordan, and then north until he was adjacent to Jericho, across the Jordan River. Here on "the plains of Moab" he delivered his final words of counsel concerning entry into Canaan. Again, the same theme is sounded. Possession of the land is linked to covenant fidelity. To break the law is to lose the land. Note his words in Deuteronomy 4:

When you have had children and children's children, and become complacent in the land, if you act corruptly by making an idol in the form of anything, thus doing what is evil in the sight of the LORD your God, and provoking him to anger, I call heaven and earth to witness against you today that you will soon utterly perish from the land that you are crossing the Jordan to occupy; you will not live long on it, but will be utterly destroyed. The LORD will scatter you among the peoples; only a few of you will be left among the nations where the LORD will lead you. (vv. 25–27)

Keep his statutes and his commandments, which I am commanding you today for your own well-being and that of your descendants after you, so that you may long remain in the land that the LORD your God is giving you for all time. (v. 40)

Perhaps Moses' most important teachings concerning the land can be found in Deuteronomy 8–9. This is a summary of what God had done for Israel from Egypt until then. Above all, it reminds Israel to be humble when it comes to the land. The land and its wealth are gifts to be held with humility.

> Do not say to yourself, "My power and the might of my own hand have gotten me this wealth." But remember the LORD your God, for it is he who gives you power to get wealth, so that he may confirm his covenant that he swore to your ancestors, as he is doing today. If you do forget the LORD your God and follow other gods to serve and worship them, I solemnly warn you today that you shall surely perish. (Deut. 8:17–19)

The severity of these words cannot be missed. Israel cannot be cavalier about its use of the land or its abuse of its inhabitants. This land is not like any other land. The wonder of this land has little to do with its natural beauty or its powerful history. We dare not be romantic or sentimental here. With many evangelicals I often read Deuteronomy 11:11–12 in this way. "But the land that you are crossing over to occupy is a land of hills and valleys, watered by rain from the sky, a land that the LORD your God looks after. The eyes of the LORD your God are always on it, from the beginning of the year to the end of the year." What does God look for? God looks for holiness and justice among those who possess this land.

WHO REALLY OWNS THE LAND?

God's remarkable interest in the land of Israel/Palestine is easily explained. The Bible teaches that the nation of Israel does not own the land; God does.[13] God's investment in the land did not disappear when the covenant with Israel was written. Since Israel and God would live closely together in covenant relation, God and Israel together would enjoy the land. Leviticus makes this perfectly clear. As the law outlines how to use the land (tenant agreements, farming practices, purchasing land) the Israelites are reminded: "The land shall not be sold in perpetuity, for the land is mine; with me you are but aliens and tenants" (Lev. 25:23). Israel is a tenant in the land, not a landlord. Israel is a renter, a visitor, an alien. The land is "a delightful gift—owned by [God] and leased to Israel in partial fulfillment of His word of promise."[14] Israel must hold this land loosely, because God will always determine the tenure of its occupants.

One of the interesting features of the first six books of the Bible is that the phrase "the land of Israel" is never used. Instead it is called "the land of Canaan." This is striking when we consider that this land is given to Israel in these books. Thus Genesis 23:2 says, "And Sarah died at Kiriath-arba (that is, Hebron) in the land of Canaan; and Abraham went in to mourn for Sarah and to weep for her."[15] Naming is always significant in the Bible. This title for the land preserves an important reminder that the land has a heritage that is larger than Israel's own history. Its importance is not defined by the new thing God is doing in the covenant with Israel. The land has a life and identity that is independent of Israel.

God's ownership of Israel/Palestine is clarified further through the rituals of Israel's religion.

1. The land was not to be considered private property, but was something distributed by God. Therefore the whole land was divided up by the casting of lots (Num. 26:55) to make way for God's will. The divisions of land were God's decision, not that of the people of Israel.[16] It is interesting to note that the tribes were trustees of the land and not individuals (Num. 36:3; Josh. 17:5).[17] Tribal supervision of land meant that individual ownership was always mediated through some corporate body.

This notion of "loose ownership" is reinforced through the Jubilee year celebrations outlined in Leviticus 25. God's gift of land could not be bought or sold permanently as if the Israelite owner could hand on a deed. Land could never be taken forever. Long-term investments in which wealthy people would develop large estates were impossible. The land was not the occupant's to do with as he or she wished. By God's decree, every fiftieth year the land had to be returned to its original owner. He controlled who would occupy the land.

2. The harvests were understood in light of God's owner-

ship. First things such as crops and firstborn animals belonged
to God and were therefore offered to him in sacrifice (Ex. 22:28;
Lev. 18:24; Deut. 14:22; 26:9–15). These sacrifices represented
the entire yield of the land and were a ritual way of acknowledging God's ownership of the whole.

3. The command to "keep the Sabbath" (Ex. 20:8–10) was
extended to the land: "When you enter the land that I am
giving you, the land shall observe a sabbath for the LORD" (Lev.
25:2). Some have viewed this ecologically, thinking that produc-
tivity would be enhanced by giving the land rest every seventh
year. But here the sense is different. The land itself is obligated
to keep a Sabbath for the Lord. The land is almost personified
as if it too owed worship to God. This emphasis underscores
the special relationship the land has with God and, in this case,
Israel was to free the land to fulfill its obligation to its creator
and owner.

4. The land is often called a place of rest for Israel (Deut.
12:9). But curiously it is actually called God's resting place (Ps.
95:11; Isa. 6:1). "Resting place" is a technical term used to
describe the place where God's presence dwells. In the
wilderness wanderings, this is where God paused (Num. 10:33)
or where he dwelt (Ps. 132:8).

5. Naming is significant throughout the Middle East. In the
Bible Israel/Palestine is the place where "God's name dwells"
(Deut. 12:11; 14:23). Similarly God "puts his name there" (Deut.
12:5, 21; 14:24) and assures "that his name is there" (1 Kings
8:16, 29). This is a mark of ownership indicating that the land is
God's own possession.[18]

6. Finally, the land is described as "holy." In Hebrew, the
term *holy* has less to do with morality than we think. Land itself
cannot have moral qualities as people can. Holiness (Heb.,
qodesh) means separation: something separated from the common world by its relationship to God is called holy. God dwells
in the land, and by virtue of its closeness to him, its character is
altered. Other land cannot share this quality. Other land is
"unclean land" (Amos 7:17). Thus Numbers 35:34 warns, "You
shall not defile the land in which you live, in which I also dwell;
for I the LORD dwell among the Israelites." The land reacts

violently to defilement ("otherwise the land will vomit you out for defiling it, as it vomited out the nation that was before you," Lev. 18:28) because it has a ritual quality quite separate from the life of Israel. It lives in close connection to God, and therefore God's attributes radiate through it.[19]

SUMMARY

When we try to address the question "Who owns the land?" only one answer seems appropriate: God owns the land. To be sure, the nation of Israel is promised possession of the land as an everlasting gift, but this promise is conditional; it depends on Israel's fidelity to the covenant and its stipulations. The land has a relationship with God too. It is the land where he lives, and by association with him, it is holy. Thus Israel may possess this promise of residence in the land and still be expelled from it through unfaithfulness.

Israel is a tenant, not an owner: "The land is mine—with me you are but aliens and tenants" (Lev. 25:23). Therefore humility and gratitude and caution should hallmark anyone's residence in the land. As God's tenants, Abraham's descendants are called to reflect God's goodness and thereby bless those who live in community with them. As we shall see, aliens or sojourners (non-Israelites) are protected and respected in this land.

We began this chapter with the account of St. John's Greek Orthodox Hospice in the Christian Quarter of Jerusalem. Does the Bible's promise of land empower men and women to take land unjustly? Does divine privilege mean that fairness may be thrown to the wind? Must the heirs of these promises exemplify goodness as a part of their inheritance? Should they be a blessing so that through them "all the families of the earth shall be blessed"?

As we shall see in the next chapter, Israel's own history tested God's expectations. The Israelites wanted the land but held no regard for the covenant or their relationship with God.

NOTES

1. Both the Armenian and the "Christian" quarters are Christian. The former is dominated by the Armenian Orthodox Church and the latter mainly by the Greek Orthodox Church. Armenia was the first nation to embrace Christianity (fourth century A.D.). Even though it disappeared as a nation, Armenians have remained an important Christian presence in the Middle East. In the early twentieth century they suffered under a systematic massacre when the Turks killed more than 2 million of them.

2. "Christians in Israel Express Their Unease," *The Christian Century* 107 (April 25, 1990): 419–20. Cf. "Palestinian Christians Fear for the Future," *Christianity Today,* August 20, 1990, 43.

3. I know a Palestinian student named Nakhleh Hussary. His father is called Abu Nakhleh. Abu in Arabic means "father of."

4. Typically, see G. von Rad, *The Problem of the Hexateuch and Other Essays* (New York: McGraw-Hill, 1966), 83–84.

5. C. Westermann, "Promise to the Patriarchs," in K. Crim, ed., *The Interpreter's Dictionary of the Bible,* supplemental volume (Nashville: Abingdon, 1962), 690–93; also R. Ruether and H. Ruether, *The Wrath of Jonah. The Crisis of Religious Nationalism in the Israeli-Palestinian Conflict* (New York: Harper & Row, 1989), 7.

6. C. Chapman, *Whose Promised Land?* (Herts, Eng.: Lion, 1983), 100–101.

7. In the New Testament even the apostle Paul makes this appeal. In Romans 11:28–29 he admits that the Jews have been "the enemies of the gospel," but for the sake of their ancestors, "they are beloved."

8. In fact, through his concubine Keturah, Abraham became the father of many North Arabian tribes. See Genesis 25:1, 4; 1 Chronicles 1:32.

9. The details of the passage underscore how carefully land transactions are understood in the Middle East: trees, caves, springs, irregularities, and all assets are commonly itemized.

10. In Galatians 3:8 Paul interprets the blessing of Abraham as referring to Christ. From this vantage, since Christ has come Genesis 12:2–3 has been fulfilled and Israel's task of "blessing" is complete.

11. W. Eichrodt, *Theology of the Old Testament,* 2 vols. (Philadelphia: Westminster, 1961, 1967), 1:457–67; W. Kaiser, *Toward an Old Testament Theology* (Grand Rapids: Zondervan, 1978), 182–219.

12. J. F. Walvoord, *Armageddon, Oil, and the Middle East Crisis* (Grand Rapids: Zondervan, 1990). Walvoord does refer to the condition of obedience (p. 71) but believes it applies only to the occupation

under Joshua and is not a feature of the covenant itself. He completely overlooks the balance of the Torah and all of the prophets.

13. "Never in Israel's history did she ever own outright the land, earth, or soil in our sense of the word; it was always granted to her by Yahweh [God] as a fief in which she could cultivate and live on it as long as she served him" (Kaiser, *Toward on Old Testament Theology*, 126).

14. Ibid., 127.

15. In the English Bible "land of Canaan" appears sixty-two times while "land of Israel" appears twenty-nine times.

16. In Numbers 27:21 we learn that the priest cast lots with "the Urim and Thummim" that he kept in his vestments. These judgments by lot were considered to be God's commands for his people. On lots, see R. deVaux, *Ancient Israel: Its Life and Institutions*, trans. J. McHugh (New York: McGraw-Hill, 1962), 352ff.; also W. D. Davies, *The Gospel and the Land. Early Christianity and Jewish Territorial Doctrine* (Berkeley: Univ. of California Press, 1974), 27–28.

17. G. von Rad, *The Problem of the Hexateuch and Other Essays* (New York: McGraw-Hill, 1966), 86.

18. Kaiser, *Toward an Old Testament Theology*, 133–34.

19. Davies, *Gospel and the Land*, 29; also, W. D. Davies, *The Territorial Dimension of Judaism* (Berkeley: Univ. of California Press, 1982), 17–21.

Chapter Four

THE NATION
AND THE LAND

> When an alien resides with you in your land, you shall not
> oppress the alien. The alien who resides with you shall be to
> you as the citizen among you; you shall love the alien as
> yourself, for you were aliens in the land of Egypt: I am the
> LORD your God. (Lev. 19:33)

> Then Solomon took a census of all the aliens who were
> residing in the land of Israel, after the census that his father
> David had taken; and there were found to be one hundred
> fifty-three thousand six hundred. (2 Chron. 2:17)

Beth Shean is one of the most spectacular sites in
Israel/Palestine. Located on the east end of the Jezreel Valley, it
was a fortress that protected one of the main access routes into
the region. King Saul lost his life in battle here. When he died,
his body was hung on the city's walls. Today a tremendous
archeological tell marks the spot, and excavations continue
annually.

In New Testament times Greeks and Romans built a city
here. Called Scythopolis, it was a major city, boasting one of
the largest theaters and horse racing tracks in the country. No
doubt Jesus passed through its streets as he traveled between
Galilee and Jerusalem.

For centuries a Palestinian town here has been called
Beisan to recall its Old Testament heritage.[1] Primarily Muslim,

70

Beisan also had a significant Christian Palestinian community—
that is, until 1948.

Naim Stifan Ateek was eleven years old in 1948.[2] He and
his family belonged to the Anglican Christian community in
Beisan. Their home was a locus of Christian activity: Bible
studies, visiting missionaries, and Sunday school classes met
there. His father even helped build an Anglican church for
Beisan. In the absence of a resident Anglican pastor (who came
from Nazareth once a month for Holy Communion), Naim's
father served as the church's lay reader.

On May 12, 1948 (two days before the state of Israel was
declared), Israeli soldiers occupied Beisan. There was no
fighting, no resistance, no killing. It was simply taken over.
After searching the homes for weapons and radios, on March
26 they rounded up the leading men of the town to make an
important announcement. Everyone would have to leave their
homes in a few hours. "If you do not leave, we will have to kill
you," they said.

When the people had gathered in the center of town, the
soldiers separated the Muslims from the Christians. The
Muslims were sent east to Jordan, and the Christians were put
on buses and deposited on the outskirts of Nazareth. Within a
few hours, Naim's mother, father, seven sisters, and two
brothers were refugees. They had lost everything except the
things they could carry. In Nazareth they joined some friends,
and seventeen of them lived in two rooms near "Mary's Well."
Naim's father went to work at once helping relief efforts for the
countless Christians and Muslims flooding Nazareth daily as
refugees.

Ten years later in 1958 the government permitted many of
the Palestinian families to travel for one day without restriction.
Naim's father was eager to bring his children to Beisan so that
they could see their "home." The Anglican church had become
a storehouse. The Roman Catholic church was a school. The
Greek Orthodox church was in ruins. Naim remembers the
moment his father stepped up to the door of his home, the one
he had built with his own hands. He wanted to see it one last
time. But his request was refused. The new Israeli occupant
said, "This is not your house. It is ours."

A few years ago I visited Beisan and thought about the beauty of this place. I was troubled that the ancient community had been uprooted at gunpoint and was now gone.

About eleven miles west of Beisan there was another beautiful place called Jezreel (the city from which the valley takes its name). Tucked under the shoulder of Mount Gilboa (an outcropping of Samaria), Jezreel had good land, good water, and excellent access to the all-important Jezreel Valley. Once in the Old Testament, an Israelite king coveted a vineyard in Jezreel in the same manner that Beisan was coveted by the Israelis. In a similar manner, the king took it. And God sent his prophet Elijah to severely rebuke the leader of God's people. In a moment (p. 83) we will turn to this story, because it powerfully tells us about land and justice. When land is occupied, does the Bible not respect the rights or honor of the people who have lived there for centuries?

JOSHUA'S CONQUEST

The book of Joshua is required reading in Israeli schools today. It holds an important place because in its pages many people think that a precedent can be found for the establishment of Israel as a nation.[3] Once I was having dinner at an evangelical graduate school on Mount Zion in Jerusalem. Speaking with a group of pastors and students, I wondered how we as Christians could explain Israel's taking of land in the "Occupied Territories." I was surprised to hear many of them agree that Joshua's conquest set a legitimate precedent and pattern for the modern day.

The instructions given to Joshua and the people of Israel before they enter the land are quite explicit. Read carefully the words of Moses as he explains what they are to do upon entering Canaan:

> 'When the LORD your God brings you into the land that you are about to enter and occupy, and he clears away many nations before you—the Hittites, the Girgashites, the Amorites, the Canaanites, the Perizzites, the Hivites, and the Jebusites, seven nations mightier and more numerous

than you—and when the Lord your God gives them over to you and you defeat them, then you must utterly destroy them. Make no covenant with them and show them no mercy. Do not intermarry with them, giving your daughters to their sons or taking their daughters for your sons, for that would turn away your children from following me, to serve other gods. Then the anger of the Lord would be kindled against you, and he would destroy you quickly. But this is how you must deal with them: break down their altars, smash their pillars, hew down their sacred poles, and burn their idols with fire. For you are a people holy to the Lord your God. . . ." (Deut. 7:1–6)

Paragraphs such as this are troubling. It seems as if Joshua is commanded to pursue a policy of genocide in order to rid Canaan of its inhabitants. How does this compare with God's command elsewhere to value and protect human life? Even Jonah was commanded to preach to the Assyrians (whose life was no better than the Canaanites). But no such suggestion comes in Joshua. This seems to be a cavalier, sweeping disposal of an entire people.[4] Three observations are necessary:

1. The battles in Joshua are aimed at coalitions of kings from the north and the south who realize that their sovereignty over Canaan is in jeopardy. Note Joshua 9:1–2:

Now when all the kings who were beyond the Jordan in the hill country and in the lowland all along the coast of the Great Sea toward Lebanon—the Hittites, the Amorites, the Canaanites, the Perizzites, the Hivites, and the Jebusites—heard of this, they gathered together with one accord to fight Joshua and Israel.

Joshua fights and destroys urban areas that exhibit military resistance to his arrival. There is no suggestion that Joshua ever massacres or depopulates large regions that did not join one of these armies. In fact, only three Canaanite cities are burned to the ground: Jericho, Ai, and Hazor. There is no Canaanite holocaust.

2. Moses' words have in mind the corrupting religious influences of the Canaanites. Note how Deuteronomy 7:5 underscores the obliteration of Canaanite religion: "But this is

how you must deal with them: break down their altars, smash their pillars, hew down their sacred poles, and burn their idols with fire." This was a fertility religion that was devoted to snake worship, the sacrifice of children, and cult prostitution. According to many scholars, it had no moral interest at all. The Canaanites were not errant believers in God. Rather their culture had reached the depths of pagan depravity.

3. Joshua treats many of the Canaanites with respect. In Jericho Rahab was not an Israelite, yet because she aided the spies and feared their God, she was protected and her life was preserved (Josh. 2). Further, even though Joshua is commanded to make no covenant with these people, he is tricked by the people of Gibeon to make such a pact. Even though Joshua erred, even though the Gibeonites were dishonest, still, Joshua keeps his word and preserves the Gibeonites (Josh. 9). In 10:6–8 Joshua even enters a battle to protect them from an attack by a five-king coalition. The significance of this event cannot be missed. Israelites risked their lives to protect Canaanites who were about to be destroyed by hostile armies! If covenants conceived in deception are respected, so too would be covenants conceived in goodwill.

This acceptance of non-Israelites is also seen when Joshua first enters the land, and he requires that the people renew their commitment to the covenant in the central mountains (on the mountains of Ebal and Gerizim, Josh. 8:30–35). The audience participating in this renewal ceremony consisted of Israelites and non-Israelites. Residents who were foreign to Israel's history stood beneath the blessings and curses of the law. This is surprising if only Israelites were permitted to enjoy this land and God's covenant.

> And afterward [Joshua] read all the words of the law, blessings and curses, according to all that is written in the book of the law. There was not a word of all that Moses commanded that Joshua did not read before all the assembly of Israel, and the women, and the little ones, *and the aliens who resided among them.* (Josh. 8:34–35. *Emphasis added.*)

4. Joshua never drives out all of the Canaanites. Joshua 13 lists those areas that remained under Canaanite control. In addition, we know that Jerusalem was never conquered by the tribe of Judah: "But the people of Judah could not drive out the Jebusites, the inhabitants of Jerusalem; so the Jebusites live with the people of Judah in Jerusalem to this day" (Josh. 15:63). Curiously, Joshua 12:10 says clearly that the king of Jerusalem was defeated and his army destroyed when he joined a southern coalition of forces arrayed against Israel (10:3–5, 22–27). And yet the Jebusites who lived in Jerusalem (who were now without military defense) were left alone. Why did Joshua not storm Jerusalem and take it?

To sum up, the portrait given in Joshua is not as uniform as we might think. City-fortresses hostile to Joshua suffer a devastating defeat, but not every Canaanite life is expunged from the land. Indeed, significant areas, particularly in Galilee near Mount Hermon, the coast of Lebanon, and the foothills inhabited by Philistines remain in Canaanite control.

The parallel between Joshua's conquest and the modern Israeli occupation of the land is inappropriate. Joshua's mandate applied to a specific historic period of time when the Canaanites promoted a religion utterly inimical to God's law. Modern Israel/Palestine is populated by people—Christians and Muslims—many of whom have a deep reverence for the Lord God of Abraham. In fact, Rahab's spiritual disposition was not unlike that of the Palestinians who acknowledge and worship the same God as the Jews but are not Jewish themselves.

CRISIS AMONG THE JUDGES

After the conquest, the Israelite tribes settle in their designated territories and begin to enjoy the land God had promised to them. However, Judges tells us through a cycle of stories that each generation of people willfully neglects the covenant and then is brought under God's judgment. Judges 3:7–8 is typical:

The Israelites did what was evil in the sight of the LORD,
forgetting the LORD their God, and worshiping the Baals and
the Asherahs. Therefore the anger of the LORD was kindled
against Israel, and he sold them into the hand of King
Cushan-rishathaim of Aram Naharaim; and the Israelites
served Cushan-rishathaim eight years.

In response to their prayers for mercy, God raises up a judge
(such as Ehud, Deborah, Gideon, or Samson) who leads Israel
to victory. This results in a period of national peace in which
correct worship is restored (generally for forty years) until the
next generation enters the scene.

This much of Judges is well known. However, the book
concludes with two troubling stories that serve as a summary of
the evil that is growing in the land. The final verse of the book
epitomizes Israel's condition: "In those days there was no king
in Israel; all the people did what was right in their own eyes"
(Judg. 21:25). Judges 17–21 describes the fallenness of the tribes
of Dan and Benjamin in parallel terms.

The story of Dan illustrates Israel's religious corruption
(chaps. 17–18). Dan leaves its territory in the western coastal
hills (the Shephelah), travels north through the central mountains of "Samaria," and meets a priestly assistant (a Levite) in
Ephraim and offers him a job as tribal priest.[5] They said to him,
"Come with us, and be to us a father and a priest." The tribe
resettles in the far north near Mount Hermon and there
establishes a new religion based on this new priest's idol.
Spearheaded by six hundred men of Dan, this is an utter
rejection of God's covenant, apostasy and religious corruption
in its worst form.

The story of Benjamin illustrates Israel's moral corruption
(chaps. 19–21). As the final story of Judges, it is meant to shock
and sober. Once again a Levite takes center stage. Because his
young concubine had fled home to her father in Bethlehem, the
Levite goes there to recover her. He then travels with her north,
en route no doubt to Shiloh, where he assists the priests.
Because nightfall has come, he seeks lodging in Gibeah, a city
of the tribe of Benjamin. After an elderly man takes them in,
that night men of Gibeah pound on the door. They wish to rape

the Levite (19:22). The host offers his virgin daughters instead but to no avail. Then the Levite throws his young concubine out the door, and she is raped by the group of men throughout the night. In the morning the Levite finds her on the doorstep and gives her an order to get up, but she is dead.

He then chops her body into a dozen parts and ships them to each tribe. Outraged by the immorality of Gibeah, the tribes descend, attacking Benjamin and killing all but six hundred men; and then lest tribal Benjamin become extinct, they kidnap wives for them at Jabesh-Gilead (after slaughtering the rest of the city) and Shiloh (where God is worshiped). This is moral anarchy and sexual violence unlike anything witnessed before.[6]

These two parallel stories make an important point.[7] In chapter 3 we learned that God's blessing of land was dependent on fidelity to the covenant. What was implicit in the law, Judges now shows in reality: *sinfulness results in the loss of inheritance.* Dan neglects its promised land in the Shephelah and migrates into apostasy in the far reaches of the north. Tribal Benjamin almost disappears from history because it has lost any sense of God's moral commands. Its sin as well as that of the Levite are simply heinous.

Land and righteousness are linked. When each generation neglects the covenant, the land is conquered by a foreign power. When a specific tribe offends the covenant, its promises are placed in jeopardy. Joshua had reminded the people that this would happen. When they first entered the land, recall that he gathered them at Mount Ebal and Mount Gerizim and read the law once again aloud. He reminded them that the covenant did not simply bring privilege; it brought expectation. It brought the prospects for both blessing and judgment at the same time.

ISRAEL'S KINGS

Throughout Judges and 1 Samuel, the people of Israel insist on having a king (cf. the offer to Gideon, Judg. 8:22ff.). While they think that this will enhance their nationhood, the prophet Samuel warns that just the opposite will happen (1 Sam. 8). To have a human king is to reject God as king—and this will lead to neglect of the covenant. Kings, Samuel argues, bring war (vv. 10–12) and taxes (vv. 15–18). They will consume the young who are seduced into serving the "empire" (vv. 13, 16). And, interestingly, they will steal the land (v. 14).

It would be a mistake to think of the nation built by Saul, David, and Solomon as culturally monolithic, as if it were "a Jewish state" in the modern sense. Non-Jews were not marginalized or expelled. On the contrary, "ancient empires were hegemonic, not ethnically exclusive."[8] This means that different cultures were integrated into the mainstream of national life under the sovereignty of the king and his dominant nation. For instance, in 2 Samuel 4:2–3 we read that two of Saul's military captains were "Be-er'othites." This was a "foreign" or "alien" tribe, a non-Israelite people living within Saul's kingdom.

This integration of non-Israelites can be seen in King David's case by looking at the different men who populated the ranks of his military officers. Second Samuel 23 (also 1 Chron. 11:10–47) lists the core of David's military organization: three leading "champions" and thirty secondary commanders. In this list, numerous non-Israelites are included from territories conquered by David.[9] Zobah (v. 36) was in the central valley of Lebanon, Maacah (v. 34) was a Syrian kingdom above the Golan Heights,[10] and Ammon (v. 37) was on the plateau east of the Jordan River (the capital of modern-day Jordan, Amman, gets its name from this kingdom).[11] The Hittites (v. 39) came from modern-day Turkey in the distant north. Remarkably this means that David's army was led by a diversity of men, many of whom were not native Israelites. Using today's geographical terms, he enlisted men from Lebanon, Syria, Jordan, and Turkey, and they were some of his trusted leaders. David's generals and colonels were fully international.

The inclusion of the "alien" or foreigner can be seen in yet another way. Non-Israelites assisted in the construction of the temple in Jerusalem (1 Chron. 22:2). At one point Solomon took a census of the number of resident aliens in his kingdom and discovered that there were 153,600 of them (2 Chron. 2:17). After King Hezekiah cleansed and restored worship at the temple following a time of severe disbelief, he called the people to Jerusalem and led them in a Passover festival. Were foreigners invited in? Indeed. "The whole assembly of Judah, the priests and the Levites, and the whole assembly that came out of Israel, and the resident aliens who came out of the land of Israel, and the resident aliens who lived in Judah, rejoiced" (2 Chron. 30:25).

Why did Israel give such respect to these resident aliens? The answer came from Israel's own history. Israel had been alienated once in Egypt. They too had been refugees. The Israelites were commanded to give offerings from their crops to God each year. As they handed the basket of goods to the priest, they were to recite: "A wandering Aramean was my ancestor; he went down into Egypt and lived there as an alien, few in number, and there he became a great nation, mighty and populous"(Deut. 26:5; cf. Ps. 119:19). Because God had been generous with the alien Israel, so too, Israel was obligated to be generous with other foreigners. At the end of his life, when David prayed for Solomon his son, his prayer for Solomon's humility was rooted in this notion: "For we are aliens and transients before you, as were all our ancestors; our days on the earth are like a shadow, and there is no hope" (1 Chron. 29:15).

ALIENS AND SOJOURNERS IN THE LAND

Two themes are beginning to appear. First, Israel's possession of the land is linked to covenant righteousness. Possession of the land is conditioned on faithfulness to God. Thus when David gives advice to his son Solomon before the construction of God's temple begins, he says, "Now therefore in the sight of all Israel, the assembly of the LORD, and in the hearing of our God, observe and search out all the commandments of the LORD your God; that you may possess this good land, and leave it for an inheritance to your children after you forever" (1 Chron. 28:8). Keeping the land is hinged to keeping the law.

Second, one feature of righteous nationhood is Israel's fair treatment of resident aliens or foreigners—non-Israelites who were in the land before Israel arrived. Rather than being expelled, they are included in the fabric of Israelite society. In fact, Israel's population had a significant non-Israelite minority (over 150,000 people).

Let us take a closer look at the rights of these "aliens" who lived alongside the Israelites. One curiosity of the Bible is that the social fabric of ancient Israel made generous allowances for "the alien (or sojourner), the orphan, and the widow." As non-Israelites, aliens were accorded surprising privileges. They were not pushed to the outskirts of society to make way for a comprehensive Jewish state. Here is a partial list of the benefits for aliens given in the law:

1. Religious Privileges

Non-Israelites were included in religious ceremony and worship.
- Aliens enjoyed the Sabbath Rest and could not be required to work (Ex. 23:12).
- Aliens could participate in all the major festivals in Jerusalem (Num. 9:14); however, in order to participate in the Passover, the alien had to be circumcised (Ex. 12:48).
- Aliens could even make personal sacrifices at the altar for worship (Num. 15:14).
- Access to the holiest ceremonies was not restricted. For instance, when Joshua recommitted Israel to the covenant with God, aliens stood alongside Israelites near the ark (Josh. 8:33).

2. Social Privileges

Non-Israelites were cared for in "social programs" that assisted the needy.
- The Israelites were commanded not to harvest their fields thoroughly so that aliens, orphans, and widows could take freely what was left (Lev. 19:10; 23:27; Deut. 24:19–21).
- When the tithes were collected (these functioned like modern taxes), the income was also to be distributed to the aliens, orphans, and widows so that their lives could be blessed with material sustenance (Deut. 14:29; 26:12).
- The law protected anyone from falling into permanent slavery through indebtedness. Means of redemption were extended to all, including the alien (Lev. 25:47–50). This

protected the social and financial future of the non-Israelite family.

3. *Legal Privileges*

Non-Israelites were to have access to the same system of justice enjoyed by the Israelites.

- Israel had a system of "cities of refuge" throughout the land which kept people from being victimized by revenge. The accused could flee there to find protection and justice. Aliens could use these cities without restriction (Num. 35:15; Josh. 20:9).
- Wages had to be fair, and none could be withheld from the alien (Deut. 24:14).
- Similarly, aliens could not be oppressed or discriminated against as if they were not full citizens. Leviticus 19:33–34 is explicit: "When an alien resides with you in your land, you shall not oppress the alien. The alien who resides with you shall be to you as the citizen among you; you shall love the alien as yourself, for you were aliens in the land of Egypt: I am the LORD your God."
- The court system available to Israelites was to be available to aliens. There were not to be two systems of justice (Deut. 1:16; 24:17). Note the tone of Deuteronomy 27:19: "Cursed be anyone who deprives the alien, the orphan, and the widow of justice. All the people shall say, Amen!"
- The Bible repeats numerous times that there was to be one law that applied to all people. Aliens and Israelites were not to obey different legal codes. No law could bind aliens unless it was also binding on Israelites (Lev. 24:22; Num. 9: 14; 15:16, 29).

The resulting conclusion is inescapable. Israel was commanded to create a remarkable society. And one test of its goodness was the way the foreigner, the alien, or the non-Israelite was treated.

TWO STORIES, TWO KINGS

Respect for anyone who owns land—including the resident alien—and the righteous requirements of possessing the land come together in two important Old Testament stories. In each case, an Israelite desires land. In each case, he has to make a moral choice about how to treat the person who owns it.

In 1 Chronicles 21 King David is instructed to build an altar for God on a small hill just north of David's Jerusalem. This place was going to become the site of Solomon's glorious temple (1 Chron. 22:1–5), and therefore an angel even points out the exact location (21:18, 20). Thus if the land belongs to God, surely this plot of land is especially his! If David is to be the steward of the whole land, this plot will be at the center of Israel's inheritance. This temple will be God's own house, the symbolic place of his dwelling with his people.

But there is one problem. The chosen site is a threshing floor owned by a man named Ornan, a Canaanite resident of pre-Israelite Jerusalem when the city was called "Jebus." Ornan "the Jebusite" is among those people listed in Genesis 15:20–21 whose land would be inherited by Israel. If David, the conqueror of Jebus/Jerusalem, had taken the land unilaterally from Ornan, it would not surprise us. Israel had inherited that threshing floor. But note what happens. Ornan tries to give it to David freely, along with a yoke of oxen for a sacrifice, but the king refuses the gift. "No," David responds; "I will buy them for the full price. I will not take for the LORD what is yours, nor offer burnt offerings that cost me nothing" (1 Chron. 21:24). David then pays six hundred shekels of gold for the site.

This story is interesting because it records that David dealt justly with Ornan the Jebusite when trying to obtain land that was precious and valued. If any land was "God's land," it was this threshing floor. Yet David did not take it at "spear point." As champion of God's covenant, David showed justice and righteousness in how he acquired it.

In 1 Kings 21 we find a different sort of story. King Ahab possessed a second palace in the Jezreel Valley not far from the Arab town of Beisan mentioned at the beginning of this chapter. Adjoining the king's property was a beautiful vineyard owned by Naboth, a longtime resident of this land. King Ahab offered to buy the vineyard, but Naboth refused to sell. Money was not the issue; this land had been in Naboth's family for generations. His history and heritage were at stake. For

Naboth, this land was sacred and deeply loved. The king even offered Naboth an alternative vineyard somewhere else, but Naboth was not interested.

Ahab's wife, Jezebel, had the perfect solution. Since Naboth would not move, she would have him accused unjustly and then murdered. At a public ceremony, scoundrels hired by Jezebel charge Naboth with cursing both God and the king.

After the elders stone Naboth to death, Ahab quickly moves in and takes possession of the vineyard. But this is not the end of the story. In the very next paragraph God calls the prophet Elijah to deliver this message: "Thus says the LORD: Have you killed, and also taken possession? Thus says the LORD: In the place where dogs licked up the blood of Naboth, dogs will also lick up your blood" (1 Kings 21:19). Shortly thereafter, Ahab is killed in battle.

This story is crucial for our study because it shows God's uncompromising concern for justice among his people as they possess the land.[12] Naboth's rights must be protected. When justice is flouted, God's judgment is swift. Naim Ateek, the Palestinian pastor from Beisan, comments on the Naboth story: "[God's] ethical law, championed by the prophets, operated impartially: every person's rights, property, and very life were under divine protection." Whenever injustice occurred, God intervened to defend the poor, the weak, and the defenseless.[13]

In 1966 an Arab peasant asked an official at the Israel Lands Administration, "How do you deny my right to this land? It is my property. I inherited it from my parents and grandparents, and I have the deed of ownership." The official replied, "Ours is a more impressive deed; we have the deed for the land from Dan [in the far north] to Elat [in the far south]." Another official was paying a peasant a token sale price for his land. Holding the peasant's property deed, the official remarked, "This is not your land; it is ours, and we are paying you 'watchman's wages,' for that is what you are. You have watched our land for two thousand years, and now we are paying your fee. But the land has always been ours."[14]

SUMMARY

The Bible is not ambiguous when it describes how God's people must live when they reside in his land. They must pursue justice and integrity at all costs. Further, the treatment of resident aliens is one test of their national character. To abuse non-Israelites is to neglect God's commitment to the underprivileged and the alien. To live unrighteously is to ignore God's covenant. And to mistreat the alien by taking his land places Israel's inheritance in jeopardy. While the covenant promises to Abraham are forever, those who inherit and enjoy these blessings must live righteously in order to keep them.

NOTES

1. *Beisan* is derived etymologically from *Beth Shean*.

2. The personal story of Naim Ateek is told in full in his excellent book *Justice and Only Justice* (Maryknoll, N.Y.: Orbis, 1989), 7–17. In it, Ateek describes the dilemma of being Palestinian, Arab, Christian, and an Israeli citizen. Today Ateek is the pastor of the Arabic-speaking congregation of St. George's Anglican Cathedral in East Jerusalem.

3. A comprehensive study of Joshua noting its implications for modern Israel has been written by a Palestinian pastor in the Arab Anglican church. See Zahi Nassir, "The Israelite Conquest of Palestine. Theological Implications for Claiming a Land" (unpublished B.Div. diss., Baptist Theological Seminary, Rüschlikon, Switzerland, 1987). See also A. Rantisi, *Blessed Are the Peacemakers. A Palestinian Christian in the Occupied West Bank* (Grand Rapids: Zondervan, 1990), 157ff.

4. Some scholars resolve this problem by disputing the historical accuracy of Joshua's conquest story. Many believe that the Israelites migrated into Canaan gradually, engaged in various local conflicts, and later became the dominant culture. The conquest account, in their view, has been read back into history from centuries later.

5. Not only was it wrong for the Levite to promote idol worship, but a Levite was never permitted to serve as priest. At this time priestly worship was conducted only at the town of Shiloh in the north central mountains of Israel. Ironically Shiloh is quite near where the Danites recruited the Levite.

6. This story intentionally echoes the account of Lot in Sodom (Gen. 19). There the two visiting angels are threatened with homosexual rape and Lot offers his two daughters. Because of the hostility of

Sodom, the angels destroy the city with fire after Lot's family is told to flee.

7. Note their parallels: a Levite, six hundred men, profound sin in the central hill country, and violation of the covenant. Dan was one of Israel's least significant tribes. Benjamin was deemed the most privileged since its forefather (Benjamin) was the youngest and last son of Rachel, Jacob's favored wife.

8. R. Ruether and H. Ruether, *The Wrath of Jonah. The Crisis of Religious Nationalism in the Israeli-Palestinian Conflict* (New York: Harper & Row, 1989), 9.

9. See J. Mauchline, *1 and 2 Samuel*, The New Century Bible (London: Oliphants, 1971), 320–21. Note that the young man who mercifully killed the wounded King Saul and brought David Saul's crown was "a resident alien, an Amalekite" (2 Sam. 1:13).

10. In 2 Samuel 10:6–14 we have an account of mercenaries from Maacah fighting against David and suffering defeat.

11. The Ammonites descended from Lot (Gen. 19:38). Even though the Ammonites did not inherit the land promises (since they did not descend from Abraham), still, Deuteronomy 2:19 required that they be treated with honor.

12. The story itself has become a model for biblical justice, a key for unlocking the Bible for Palestinian Christians like Naim Ateek, who once lived in Beisan. For many Palestinian believers, Israel has been guilty of the sin of Ahab. See Ateek's comments, *Justice and Only Justice*, 86–89.

13. Ibid., 88.

14. Report by the attorney Hannah Nakkara in *Al Ittihad*, July 15, 1966. Cited in Sabri Jiryis, *The Arabs in Israel*, trans. from Arabic by Inea Bushnaq (New York: Monthly Review Press, 1976), 74.

Chapter Five

THE PROPHETS AND THE LAND

For if you truly amend your ways and your doings, if you truly act justly one with another, if you do not oppress the alien, the orphan, and the widow, or shed innocent blood in this place, and if you do not go after other gods to your own hurt, then I well dwell with you in this place, in the land that I gave of old to your ancestors forever and ever. (Jer. 7:5–7)

The Palestinian village of Beita (pronounced *beta*) has stood for centuries in a remote section of the hills of Samaria between Jerusalem and biblical Shechem (Nablus today). Electricity came to Beita ten years ago. Water is still drawn from the village well. Life here is hard.

Nearby is the Israeli settlement of Elon Moreh. Well scrubbed, beautiful, modern, and heavily guarded, Elon Moreh was built in these hills just a few years ago much to the dismay of the Arabs who live nearby. The tile roofs and gardens of Elon Moreh make it look like a patch of San Diego lifted from California and set in Israel.

On Friday, April 6, 1988, tragedy struck. It was Passover season, and Israel was celebrating its fortieth anniversary. Sixteen teenagers from Elon Moreh were hiking by Beita with two armed civilian guards.[1] They said they were on a picnic— and so the press reported it—but, as the village *mukthar*, or mayor, told me later, "No Israelis come to this little hill for a picnic." He was right. Tension between the village and the settlement had been strong for some time. And Beita was no picnic area.

When the group of eighteen approached the village, one of the guards, Romam Aldubi, age twenty-six, fired his M-16 at a village farmer who was plowing his field. The farmer died within the hour. Another farmer, Tasir Saleh, was called over. When he asked, "What do you want with our village?" he was shot point blank in the stomach by the same guard with the M-16.[2] When the mother and sister of the first farmer discovered the death of their loved one, they rushed at the Israelis, throwing stones.

Suddenly a mob formed. Arab teenagers from Beita began throwing stones by hand and with slings at the Israeli teenagers. The Arab village men tried to intervene and protect the Israeli teenagers. One girl from Elon Moreh, Rachely Savitiz, later told how an Arab family grabbed her and hid her in their home for protection. As the group neared the village, the two Israeli guards opened fire with their automatic weapons, and bullets flew everywhere. One Arab boy fell dead.[3] Another fled across the field and was killed by a bullet in his back.[4] Two other Arabs were wounded. And then one of the Israeli girls, a fifteen-year-old teenager named Tirza Porat, fell dead from a bullet wound to the head. She was the first Israeli casualty since the Intifada began. No one knew who fired the shot. Aldubi became crazed and wanted to machine gun the crowd of villagers, but the other Israeli guard stopped him.

Arab villagers grabbed the two armed men to pacify them and took their M-16 rifle and Uzzi submachine gun. They removed the ammunition clips and tried to break the guns, slamming them on the ground.[5] Other villagers continued to protect the Israeli teenagers from harm during the melee and transported any who were hurt to a medical facility in Nablus.

Immediately hundreds of Israeli soldiers descended on Beita and sealed it off. Even Arab ambulances from Nablus were not permitted in. At once house-to-house searches began in an attempt to find the murderers of the Israeli girl. The following nine days shocked the Middle East and the world.

For three days, Beita earned front-page headlines in the *New York Times*.[6]

Thursday, April 7. *Jerusalem Post* headlines: "Settler girl stoned to death." Elon Moreh buries Tirza Porat at a nationally watched funeral while hundreds of soldiers chant, "Revenge, revenge. Expel the Arabs." One speaker from Elon Moreh promises to build another settlement near Beita in the dead girl's name. Prime Minister Yitzhaq Shamir speaks at the funeral, promising that revenge will be had. "God will revenge her blood," he says. Rabbi Chaim Druckman also speaks: "The village of Beita should be wiped from the face of the earth." The minister of justice, Avraham Sharir, recommends that dozens of Beita homes be destroyed and hundreds of the residents be exiled to Lebanon.

That afternoon helicopters search the hills looking for hiding Arab youths. One is found running and is shot and killed without being identified. The army blows up four Beita homes of Arabs suspected of violence, though no evidence is provided that the inhabitants are guilty. In Hawara village, one mile away from Beita, armed Israeli settlers rampage through the streets breaking car windshields and windows in homes. The army looks on.

On Thursday evening Israeli television runs lurid photographs of the Israeli girl's body. Public outcry against Beita grows dramatically throughout Israel. Beita becomes a "media event."

Friday, April 8. The Israeli army blows up eight more homes in Beita without conducting any formal trial or investigation. The Israeli army's autopsy says that the bullet that killed the girl was from the same gun that killed the Arab youths on that Wednesday. This suggests that an Israeli guard killed her by accident. Israeli chief of staff, General Dan Shomron, remarks, "The Arab residents of Beita had intended no harm to the Elon Moreh hikers." The settlers of Elon Moreh, reject this report angrily. Increased Arab demonstrations break out in nearby Nablus, and forty-nine Arab youths are injured.

Israeli soldiers ransack the central hospital in Nablus looking for injured Beita residents. Doctors and nurses are locked in an office, and numerous patients are beaten. The next day, the hospital staff stages a protest.

Saturday, April 9. Fourteen more houses in Beita are marked for demolition. Thirty people have been arrested in connection with Wednesday's incident. Sixty-five homes in Beita are damaged by soldiers. Since it is the Sabbath, the day is quiet.

Sunday, April 10. Israeli defense minister, Yitzhaq Rabin, confirms publicly that the girl died from a gunshot fired by Romam Aldubi, one of the Israeli guards. Aldubi's profile is released: a militant follower of radical Rabbi Meir Kahane, Aldubi had fired on Palestinians at Balata refugee camp outside Nablus and had been banned from entering Nablus again or serving in the army. Still, he owned an army-issued M-16. Rabin identifies Aldubi as the culprit.

Hours later the army announces that it plans to expel from the country six Beita youths connected with the incident. They have received no trial. They will be deposited by helicopter in southern Lebanon never to return home again.

A high-ranking army officer comes to the village and speaks in confidence with the mukthar of Beita. He apologizes secretly for what the army is doing to the village. The homes are being destroyed to appease the outraged Israeli settlers.

Israel's trade minister, Ariel Sharon, recommends publicly that all Beita residents be expelled and every home in the village be destroyed.

The Israeli Supreme Court bars any further destruction of Beita homes. Israeli newspapers *Ha'Aretz* and *Hadashot* call for a stop to the punishment of Beita. *Hadashot* calls it an attempt to pacify the settlers of Elon Moreh.

Monday, April 11. Israeli chief of staff, General Dan Shomron, is criticized by the settlers because he praises the people of Beita for protecting the Elon Moreh teenagers during the conflict. Some in the Israeli Parliament call for his resignation. Still, the army blows up two more homes, destroys Beita's grove of almond trees, and uproots hundreds of its ancient olive trees. No trial has yet been held for anyone in Beita.

The United Nations Security Council adopts a resolution—

supported by the United States—condemning Israel's expulsion of Palestinians.

Charles Redman, a spokesman for the U.S. State Department, reiterates the U.S. government's position: deportations violate the Geneva International Human Rights Agreements, which Israel signed.

Tuesday, April 12. United Nations secretary general, Javier Perez de Cuellar, publicly criticizes Israeli actions concerning Beita and the deportations. Britain likewise makes a public condemnation. U.S. Ambassador Thomas R. Pickering, speaking at Jerusalem's Hebrew University, complains that Israel cannot continue demolishing homes, deporting Arabs, and failing to provide fair judicial process. Prime Minister Yitzhaq Shamir defends the army and warns the Palestinians that more expulsions and demolitions will occur unless they stop their hostilities.

Wednesday, April 13. The army publishes its final report on Beita, admitting that the gunshot killing the girl was indeed fired by an Israeli. Elon Moreh is responsible for the incident. However, the army has no plans to rebuild Beita's destroyed homes.

Tuesday, April 19. At 3:00 P.M. an Israeli helicopter gunship lands in southern Lebanon. Ghassan Ali Ezzat Massri, Mahmoud Jahoub, Musstafa Ayed Hamayel, Najeh Jameel Saada Dweikat, Sari Khaleel Dhaher Hamayel, Ahmad Fawzi Khaled Deek, Omar Muhammad Saud Daoud, and Ibraheem Muhammad Khidr are told to get out and never return to Israel/Palestine again. Six of these young men are from Beita. They have never seen the inside of a courtroom. They have never been defended, and they will never return home to their families again. Accused of throwing stones, they are given a life sentence of exile.

When I visited Beita about two years later and was given a tour of the destroyed homes by the village mukthar, I was saddened and angry and depressed. Soldiers had come in the following months and made Beita's men remove the debris of the homes so that the evidence of their destruction would be minimal. As I stood in the rubble of one of the homes, I picked up a piece of plaster with light green paint on it and put it in my pocket. It now sits on a shelf in my office. It is a witness, a record of violence to a people whose story has been forgotten everywhere except among the Palestinians.

The entire Old Testament links justice and the land. We have seen this in the books of law as well as in the history of Israel's kingship. When Joshua first entered the land, he renewed Israel's covenant by designating Mount Ebal and Mount Gerizim as "guardians of the covenant." The mountains would look down on the people and assess if blessings or curses should come to the Israelites.

The same can be found in the prophets. Men like Jeremiah, Amos, Isaiah, and Ezekiel had little patience for a nation that ignored righteousness as it built its empire. Kings who consumed land, who moved landmarks, and who destroyed innocent people and their homes, would soon find themselves facing a prophet just as Ahab faced Elijah. Or they would face God. Even King David, for instance, was told that he was disqualified from building God's holy temple because he had slaughtered so many people—so many foreigners—in his quest for nationhood (1 Chron. 22:8). King David had blood on his hands.

THE LAND AND THE PROPHET

Israel failed to understand that it could not be a nation like other nations. Its kings could not treat the land like other lands. This is, as Walter Brueggeman puts it, "a perennial lesson Israel had to learn and to perceive otherwise as a perennial temptation."[7] In fact, the land becomes a sort of prism that reflects the deepest values at work in Israel. The land tempts the corrupt while it encourages the righteous. The corrupt want to consume more land for more power and wealth. The righteous employ its bounty to build a better place for all.

As the land stands over against Israel like Mount Ebal towers over Shechem, assessing Israel's life in light of the covenant, so too, the prophet plays the same peculiar role. The nation is accountable to external standards. God imposes his will in the land through the prophet. To abuse and ignore the prophet is to work against the covenant and, finally, to lose the land. Kings may not appoint prophets, just as they do not write the laws of the land. Both are called into being by God, and the king and his court must conform to them obediently. This accountability makes Israel a remarkable state, an ideal state in which the imperial authorities are held to some system of justice. In Israel the king is not supreme; the law is supreme.

When the land is introduced in Deuteronomy, prophets are introduced too: "When you come into the land . . . the LORD your God will raise up for you a prophet" (Deut. 18:9–15).[8] Likewise the description of prophets follows closely on the description of kings. This may be because of the threat that kings and their governments pose. The temptation to power and corruption demands the voice of a prophet who can chasten the monarch. Deuteronomy 18:19 says, "Anyone who does not heed the words that the prophet shall speak in my name, I myself will hold accountable."

THE PROPHETS' WARNINGS

The prophets characteristically warned against the aggressive taking of land or the abuse of landowners. These were forms of heinous injustice. Note the words of Isaiah and Micah:

> Ah, you who join house to house,
>   who add field to field,
> until there is room for no one but you,
>   and you are left to live alone
>   in the midst of the land! (Isa. 5:8)

> Alas for those who devise wickedness
>   and evil deeds on their beds!
> When the morning dawns, they perform it,
>   because it is in their power.
> They covet fields, and seize them;
>   houses, and take them away;
> they oppress householder and house,
>   people and their inheritance.
> Therefore thus says the LORD:
> Now, I am devising against this family an evil
>   from which you cannot remove your necks;

and you shall not walk haughtily,
        for it will be an evil time. (Mic. 2:1–3)

These words compare with the statement of Elijah to King Ahab
when the king took the vineyard of Naboth illegally. "Have you
killed, and also taken possession?" (1 Kings 21:19). These two
offenses—murder and land seizure—would bring about the
end of Ahab's reign. His offenses would terminate his privileges in the land. The prophet Elijah guaranteed it.

Virtually every one of the Old Testament prophets echoes
the same theme. Reaching back to the covenant land promises
and the law, they point to Israel's violation of God's rule and
the necessary judgment that will follow. In each case, the land
is a vehicle of judgment. God withholds rain (Amos 4:6), sends
pestilence (4:10), and impairs the harvest (4:6) in order to
discipline his people. The land is the vehicle of disciplining.
God's ultimate judgment will be to remove the people entirely
from the land.

Speaking to the northern kingdom,[9] Amos identifies the
absence of justice in the land and announces the coming anger
of God:

> Hear this word, you cows of Bashan
>   who are on Mount Samaria,
> who oppress the poor, who crush the needy,
>   who say to their husbands,
>   "Bring something to drink!"
> The Lord GOD has sworn by his holiness:
>   The time is surely coming upon you,
> when they shall take you away with hooks,
>   even the last of you with fishhooks. (Amos 4:1–2)

Amos says that the coming judgment will result in the loss
of land:

> "Your land shall be parceled out by line;
> you yourself shall die in an unclean land,
>   and Israel shall surely go into exile away from its land."
> (Amos 7:17)

Hosea echoes the same idea. The land will refuse production to
the unrighteous. It will even reject those who abuse it:

"Threshing floor and wine vat shall not feed them,
   and the new wine shall fail them.
They shall not remain in the land of the LORD." (Hos. 9:2–
3)

Ultimately exile came in the form of Assyria's swift armies in
722 B.C., and the northern kingdom lost its inheritance because
it had lost any sense of what it meant to live under God's
covenant, "Therefore the LORD was very angry with Israel and
removed them out of his sight" (2 Kings 17:18).

The same held true for the southern kingdom with its
capital at Jerusalem. Jeremiah records how God viewed his gift
of land to Israel.

I thought
   how I would set you among my children,
and give you a pleasant land,
   the most beautiful heritage of all the nations.
And I thought you would call me, My Father,
   and would not turn from following me.
Instead, as a faithless wife leaves her husband,
   so you have been faithless to me, O house of Israel,
                        says the LORD. (Jer. 3:19–20)

Jeremiah identifies many wrongs and lists them in excruci-
ating detail. Among these he mentions the abuse of the resident
aliens who live in the land. If the orphan, the widow, and the
alien are abused, God will refuse to dwell with Israel in the
land. This does not contradict the eternal promise to Abraham—which Jeremiah acknowledges. It simply means that
these Israelites who do such things will lose the privileges of
the promise.

For if you truly amend your ways and your doings, if you
truly act justly one with another, if you do not oppress the
alien, the orphan, and the widow, or shed innocent blood in
this place, and if you do not go after other gods to your own
hurt, then I will dwell with you in this place, in the land
that I gave of old to your ancestors forever and ever. (Jer.
7:5–7)

Isaiah likewise affirms God's commitment to justice and emphasizes how the land itself will be lost if Israel does not alter its way of life.

> Wash yourselves; make yourselves clean;
> > remove the evil of your doings
> > from before my eyes;
> cease to do evil,
> > learn to do good;
> seek justice,
> > rescue the oppressed,
> defend the orphan,
> > plead for the widow. (Isa. 1:16–17)

Chapters 1–5 form a litany of complaints against the unrighteousness of the people. "Jerusalem has stumbled/ and Judah has fallen" (3:8). "They proclaim their sin like Sodom" (3:9). Moral failings stand out. "It is you who have devoured the vineyard; / the spoil of the poor is in your houses" (3:14).

It is in this setting that we find Isaiah's famous "Song of the Vineyard." Isaiah describes the good land as a vineyard tended and loved by God. And yet those whom he planted there (the Israelites) produced wild fruit, wicked fruit, unrighteous fruit that God never planned. God's decision will be to forsake the vineyard altogether:

> Let me sing for my beloved
> > my love-song concerning his vineyard:
> My beloved had a vineyard
> > on a very fertile hill.
> He dug it and cleared it of stones,
> > and planted it with choice vines;
> he built a watchtower in the midst of it,
> > and hewed out a wine vat in it;
> he expected it to yield grapes,
> > but it yielded wild grapes.
>
> And now, inhabitants of Jerusalem
> > and people of Judah,
> judge between me
> > and my vineyard.
> What more was there to do for my vineyard

that I have not done in it?
When I expected it to yield grapes,
    why did it yield wild grapes?

And now I will tell you
    what I will do to my vineyard.
I will remove its hedge,
    and it shall be devoured;
I will break down its wall,
    and it shall be trampled down.
I will make it a waste;
    it shall not be pruned or hoed,
    and it shall be overgrown with briers and thorns;
I will also command the clouds
    that they rain no rain upon it.

For the vineyard of the LORD of hosts
    is the house of Israel,
and the people of Judah
    are his pleasant planting;
he expected justice,
    but saw bloodshed;
righteousness,
    but heard a cry! (Isa. 5:1–7)

Judgment fell upon the southern kingdom in the same manner that it fell upon those in the north. In 586 B.C. Babylonian armies swept down from the north, conquered the land, destroyed Jerusalem, and carried the survivors into captivity. The inheritance of Abraham was lost.[10] The prophets simply predicted what the law had promised. Unrighteousness would lead to a loss of land.

Did Israel despair? The laments recorded following the conquest and exile are filled with longings for the land. That God would punish his people was one thing. That he would withhold the ancestral promises was quite another. Psalm 48 records the pride and overconfidence Israel possessed in the land. Since God lives in the walls of Jerusalem (48:3), no foe could dare confront Israel's national ambitions. Psalm 137 describes the shock and grief that swamped the nation when these walls were demolished by Babylonian infantry. The entire book of Lamentations wrestles with the confusion of the loss of promise. Was God's goodness compromised when he let the land be taken? No, rather Lamentations leads the reader to repentance, forgiveness, and renewal.[11]

THE PROPHETIC HOPE

If, however, possessing the land is tied to Israel's fidelity to the covenant, it is not surprising that when the prophets looked to the future, they predicted a new generation that would embrace the covenant with zeal and reclaim the land at the same time. The prophets did not simply send out a message of despair; they gave encouragement. Someday Jerusalem would be rebuilt by people who were devoted to God and who defended the justice of the covenant in the land.

Each of the prophets who predicted the judgments we have mentioned—Amos, Hosea, Isaiah, and Jeremiah— embraced this hope of restoration.[12] Hosea typically writes:

> On that day I will answer, says the LORD,
>   I will answer the heavens
>   and they shall answer the earth;
> and the earth shall answer the grain, the wine, and the oil,
>   and they shall answer Jezreel;
>   and I will sow him for myself in the land.
> And I will have pity on Lo-ruhamah,
>   and I will say to Lo-ammi, "You are my people";
>   and he shall say, "You are my God." (Hos. 2:21–23)

In these words the prophet is predicting a new harmony, not just between God and his people, but between the people and the land. God will replant Israel in the land, and the land will eagerly produce new bounty for its residents.

Of course, these predictions did come true. The Babylonians who exiled Israel were themselves defeated by the Persians, and the Persian king, Cyrus, permitted God's people to return to their land. It was another generation in another era that followed the leadership of Ezra and Nehemiah, listened to the exhortations of Haggai and Zechariah, and recommitted themselves to the unique society God had envisioned for his people.

Naim Ateek points out that the return of Israel from Babylon to Canaan is really a "second exodus" that parallels the first return from Egypt to Canaan. The first exodus is filled with negative attitudes toward the native peoples who already lived in the land. They are supposed to be destroyed. Ateek remarks: "The second [exodus] is totally different. One gets the feeling that the returning exiles reflected greater realism. They were much more accepting of the people around them."[13] This is true, yet if we read Ezra and Nehemiah carefully, we see that these people were still rigorous about their faith. Ateek then goes on to cite a crucial prophetic passage that describes this "second return":

> You shall allot it as an inheritance for yourselves and for the aliens who reside among you and have begotten children among you. They shall be to you as citizens of Israel; with you they shall be allotted an inheritance among the tribes of Israel. In whatever tribe aliens reside, there you shall assign them their inheritance, says the Lord GOD. (Ezek. 47:22–23)

As the prophets designed the contours of this future society, it is interesting that they did not leave out a place for the resident-alien, the non-Israelite. When Ezekiel describes the return to the land and its acquisition by the exiles, he specifically says that provision must be made for the non-Israelites within Israel! Note how Ezekiel echoes the words of the law (Lev. 19:34) which tell how aliens are to be treated like "fellow citizens." Aliens must have an inheritance too. And when these resident foreigners are abused or defrauded, the postexilic prophets lodge harsh complaints against Israel's leadership. Ezekiel and Malachi address the problem directly:

> Father and mother are treated with contempt in you; the alien residing within you suffers extortion; the orphan and the widow are wronged in you. . . . The people of the land have practiced extortion and committed robbery; they have oppressed the poor and needy, and have extorted from the alien without redress. (Ezek. 22:7, 29)

> Then I will draw near to you for judgment; I will be swift to bear witness against the sorcerers, against the adulterers, against those who swear falsely, against those who oppress

the hired workers in their wages, the widow and the orphan, against those who thrust aside the alien, and do not fear me, says the LORD of hosts. (Mal. 3:5)

Zechariah identifies this problem of righteousness too, but he repeats the law, the old warnings about injustice and consequences (7:10) as if to say, "Remember, the covenant and its expectations have not disappeared."

SUMMARY

The Old Testament is rigorously consistent when it comes to the land and the covenant. The prophets affirmed what the law had always said: the land of Israel/Palestine cannot become the secular possession of some secular state. This land is unlike any other land. "The eyes of the LORD your God are always on it" (Deut. 11:12). The land itself holds Israel to covenant standards of justice. Likewise the prophets hold Israel to this same standard. And when this standard is violated, judgment is sure to result.

I began this chapter by retelling the tragic story of the Palestinian village of Beita. If this were a random act of violence perpetrated by individuals—such acts are common both by Israelis and by Palestinians—then it would be easier to accept. It would then be one more example of the inexcusable violence that torments this land. What makes this episode so troubling is that the systems of Israeli justice refused to work in behalf of "the alien, the widow, and the orphan." Leading Israeli politicians, statesmen, and military officers encouraged a cycle of abuse that the world community has judged to be heinous.

What then of God's covenant with modern-day Israel? Does Israel still live under the constraints of covenant justice? If Israel makes a biblical claim to the land, then it follows that Israel must also live a biblical life, a life that resonates with the goodness God intended to create in his land.

NOTES

1. They were required to notify the local army outpost to hike here but did not. The two guards were Romam Aldubi, carrying an M-

16 automatic rifle, and Menachem Ilan, who had an Uzzi submachine gun.

2. Tasir survived and was extensively interviewed. His testimony (and that of the other Israeli eyewitnesses) was later accepted by the Israeli army as correct. See the *New York Times*, April 9, 1988, A-8.

3. Hatan Fayez Ahmed, age nineteen.

4. Mousa Abu Shalseh, age twenty.

5. The M-16 and Uzzi were later returned to the army. The M-16 still had six rounds left, which shows the danger of the elder's actions, grabbing a loaded, firing M-16.

6. The following account was carefully compiled from the following news sources which followed the Beita story daily: *The Jerusalem Post* (Israeli), *Al Nahar* (Jerusalem, Palestinian), the *New York Times*, and the wire services of Reuters and the Associated Press. With a translator I also interviewed the mukthar (village elder) of Beita as well as twelve men and one family in the village in 1990.

7. W. Brueggemann, *The Land. Place as Gift, Promise and Challenge in Biblical Faith* (Philadelphia: Fortress, 1977), 90.

8. Ibid., 91ff.

9. In 931 B.C. the tribes in the north broke away from the tribes in the south, causing a civil war in Israel. The prophets direct their chastisements to each sector of the country.

10. For a full description of the Babylonian conquest, see Jeremiah 52 and 2 Kings 24–25.

11. Today the book of Lamentations is read and sung aloud on the ninth of Av in Israel, the anniversary of the destruction of Jerusalem's temple in 586 B.C.

12. See Amos 9:14–15; Hosea 2:14–23; 11:8–11; Jeremiah 16:15; Isaiah 2:1–5; 9:1–9. Cf. Ezekiel 36–37.

13. N. Ateek, "Power, Justice and the Bible," in N. Adieux, M. Ellis, and R. Ruether, eds., *Faith and the Intifada. Palestinian Christian Voices* (Maryknoll, N.Y.: Orbis, 1992), 111.

Chapter Six

MODERN ISRAEL
IN THE LAND

"The State of Israel! My eyes filled with tears, and my hands shook. We had done it. We had brought the Jewish state into existence—and I, Golda Mabovitch Meyerson, had lived to see the day. Whatever happened now, whatever price any of us would have to pay for it, we had re-created the Jewish national home. The long exile was over." (Golda Meir, *My Life*, 226)[1]

"It should be clear that there is no room for both peoples to live in this country. . . . If the Arabs leave, it is a large and open country; if they stay, it is small and poor. Up to this point, Zionists have been content to "buy land," but this is no way to establish a country for the Jews. A nation is created in one move . . . and in that case, there is no alternative to moving the Arabs to the neighboring countries, moving them all, except, perhaps, those living in Bethlehem, Nazareth, and the Old City of Jerusalem. Not one village, not one tribe must remain. They must be moved to Iraq, Syria, or even Transjordan." (Joseph Weitz, *Diaries and Letters to the Children*, 2:181)[2]

Of the countless books published about Israel and the Middle East, two provide unparalleled insights. They are written by Jews from utterly different backgrounds.

The first is Golda Meir's autobiography, *My Life*, published in 1975.[3] Golda Meir[4] was born in 1898 into a poor Russian family. Her family emigrated to Milwaukee, Wisconsin, in 1906 when she was just a little girl. She grew up to be a passionate worker in Zionist organizations, and she and her husband moved to a kibbutz in Galilee in 1921. From a specialist in chicken raising, she became an executive member of the Jewish Administrative Agency under British rule. In 1948 she was one of the signers of Israel's Proclamation of Independence and the same year was appointed to be Israel's first ambassador to Moscow. From 1949 until 1974 she served in Israel's Parliament (the Knesset). From minister of labor (1949) she became foreign minister (1956), and in 1969 she was elected Israel's fourth prime minister. Leading her fledgling country with vigor and tenacity (foreign diplomats often received memos: "Watch out for Golda"),[5] she served with distinction until 1974, becoming known throughout the world as one of Israel's most distinguished leaders and thinkers. When she died in 1978, doctors discovered that for twelve years she had even been suffering from leukemia.

Within the pages of Golda Meir's warm and personal story, I glimpsed a view of Israel that is crucial for any student of the Middle East. She knew the persecutions and discriminations of Europe and America, and she dreamed about a Jewish homeland where anti-Semitism would no longer torment her people. She had witnessed the era of German Nazism which murdered six million of her people. As a leader in Tel Aviv, she worked to rescue her people by smuggling Jews out of Europe after World War II and buying black market weapons through secret channels. She fought with the British, haggled with the Arabs, and cut deals with American Jewish leadership. She made frequent trips to America, raising millions of dollars for her country's economy and learning the critical role the United States would play in Israel's future.

In Golda Meir's mind, the state of Israel was the historical result of centuries of anti-Semitism now wed to a vision, a Zionist vision, for a Jewish homeland. Golda Meir embraced the idea of a state where democracy and diversity and tolerance would characterize the land. And as she dreamed, she found herself bruised and embittered by Arab politicians who had no interest in a Jewish state in their corner of the world.

Nevertheless, her ideals, shaped in no small part by her biblical and Jewish traditions, remained until her retirement.

The second insightful book is Thomas Friedman's *From Beirut to Jerusalem*.[6] Friedman was born in Minneapolis in 1953 to a liberal Jewish family ("I was a three-day-a-year Jew—twice on the New Year [Rosh Hashanah] and once on the Day of Atonement [Yom Kippur]").[7] From 1979 until 1983 he worked in Beirut, Lebanon, as a reporter for UPI and later for the *New York Times*, winning the Pulitzer Prize for his coverage of the Israeli invasion of 1982. From 1984 until 1988 he wrote for the *Times* in Jerusalem, winning another Pulitzer for his outstanding work.

Friedman's passionate, intuitive, often-humorous narrative is filled with anecdotes as he describes nine years of his travels and research. But visible between the lines is his disillusionment. In fact, when he crossed from Lebanon to Israel in 1984, he found that the chaos on both sides of the border was similar. In Beirut terrorists had blown his apartment sky high while he was en route home one afternoon. In Jerusalem the demolition of his ideals was just as great.

Friedman found a country that could not decide if it was going to be a free and open democracy or an exclusive Jewish state. The former would open its doors to the Palestinians. The latter would close them. Israel had to decide. Living within its borders were over a million Arabs, wondering since 1967 what their fate would be. Full citizens with the Israelis? Free to create their own homeland? Or hostages being neither let in nor let out?

Golda Meir came to Israel/Palestine with a vision shaped by her rich Jewish traditions and the Bible. Quickly she found the vision being compromised as she played high-stakes politics with her Arab neighbors. Friedman came to Israel/Palestine hoping to find something secular, something democratic that stood out in the bitter world of Mediterranean politics. "Israelis," he learned, "cannot decide what their nation should stand for not only politically . . . but also spiritually."[8]

Meir and Friedman represent the two levels of disappointment that many of us feel as we visit and study the modern state of Israel. By comparison with other states in the Middle

East, Israel is an exemplar of moderation, civility, and freedom. When the Syrian city of Hama (population 180,000) defied the rule of President Hafez Assad, he solved the problem cleanly. At 1:00 A.M. on Tuesday, February 2, 1982, he surrounded the town with tanks and artillery and leveled the place. Assad hears little dissent today. Israel has not participated in this sort of wholesale massacre.

Yet when we look at the traditions that have shaped this country, when we look at the caliber of its leadership, we expect more. Israel is not to be compared with the tribal regimes that run Lebanon, Syria, Jordan, and Iraq. Israel seeks to be compared with the Western democracies that have shaped its political worldview. Moreover, Israel invites comparison with the biblical model of nationhood because it claims that this is the heritage that has empowered it to inherit the land.

MODERN ISRAEL AND BIBLICAL ISRAEL

The first question evangelicals have to answer is whether or not modern Israel corresponds to biblical Israel described in our Scriptures. Is this a revival of the Israelite nation, a resuscitation of the kingdom whose heritage extends back to King David, King Solomon, and King Rehoboam?

From the Israeli point of view, the answer does not take a moment's hesitation. The earliest Zionists (from Weizmann to Ben Gurion to Meir) all interpreted their work as restoring a biblical tradition even though they had secularized that tradition completely.[9] This is why, for instance, Israelis insist on calling the West Bank "Judea and Samaria." These are biblical names used to make theological and historical claim on the land. Each year the Jewish Passover service reminds worshipers to dream about "next year in Jerusalem." This liturgy has kept biblical Jerusalem in the hearts and minds of Jewish families for centuries. Likewise, it is deeply moving to witness Jews praying at the "Western Wall" (formerly the "Wailing Wall"). This mammoth section of limestone is a sought-after place of prayer because of its historic connection with the past. It is what remains of the last Jewish temple. Even army officers take their oath of office lined up on the tarmac in front of it.

Many Western Christians have likewise been eager to see in Israel a fulfillment of the prophecies that mention God's people returning to their land. This was clear even in the nineteenth century when Zionists began to first lobby for returning to the land. For instance, in 1891 William Blackstone presented a petition signed by five hundred clergy urging that Palestine be given to the Jews. Later that year he wrote:

> No other people can boast of such high authority for the title to their earthly inheritance. It is rooted in the Holy Word, which all Christian nations receive as the foundation of their religion, and the rule of their practice. Does not the present dire extremity of Israel, and the quickening of their national sentiment, and the expression of Gentile sympathy, and the providential openings toward the land, all point to the uplifted hand of God?[10]

When Israel declared its nationhood in 1948, countless writers rushed to their Bibles seeking an answer to the question of Israel and prophecy. For example, in 1958 A. W. Kac (a Jewish physician) published a full-fledged academic study asking: *The Rebirth of the State of Israel, Is It of God or of Men?*[11] In the 1960s this interest grew dramatically with the writing of scholars like John Walvoord, who proclaimed confidently that the rebirth of Israel was indeed a fulfillment of prophecy and a signal that the second coming of Jesus Christ was near.[12] Following the Israeli victory of 1967, interest in Israel was meteoric. In 1970 Hal Lindsey wrote *The Late Great Planet Earth* and, although it was hardly a well-reasoned, researched book, it caught the interest of evangelicals everywhere. Since 1970 it has sold 25 million copies.[13] In 1981 Lindsey reached the same audience with *The 1980s: Countdown to Armageddon*.[14] This little book was on the *New York Times* best-seller list for more than six months.

The linchpin in all of these writings is that modern Israel has indeed resumed the life of ancient Israel, that a direct line may be drawn between the biblical nation and the Israeli government in Jerusalem today. Calling the rebirth of Israel the "fuse of Armageddon," Lindsey spoke for countless others when he said:

With the Jewish nation reborn in the land of Palestine, ancient Jerusalem is once again under total Jewish control for the first time in 2600 years, and talk of rebuilding the great Temple, the most important prophetic sign of Jesus Christ's soon coming is before us. This has now set the stage for the other predicted signs to develop in history. It is like the key piece of a jigsaw puzzle being found and then having the many adjacent pieces rapidly fall into place.[15]

Most evangelicals have responded to this outlook by weighing the prophecies studied by Walvoord, Lindsey, and others. But their question is different from mine. *Rather than wondering if Israel is fulfilling prophecy, I prefer to grant their premise and ask a more fundamental question. Assuming for now that such continuity exists between the Old Testament and the twentieth century, how does Israel's national life compare with the life of God's people outlined in the Bible?* If Israel qualifies prophetically, does Israel also qualify ethically and morally to be God's people in the land? This was the standard of the prophets (like Amos and Isaiah) when they assessed Israel's fidelity to the covenant. As we have seen, the prophets and the land itself have specific expectations about life and nationhood. When these standards were ignored, the right to possess the land was called into question.

MODERN ISRAEL AND BIBLICAL NATIONHOOD

Evangelicals have been reluctant to open this question. But once a sensitive, reasonable person discovers just a handful of facts about Israel, the country will never be seen the same again. Most of us will say, "This can't be true" and hope to deny it. I have felt this way more than once. It is much too painful to describe but too important to ignore. Today a whole body of responsible, academic study has laid bare the character of the Israeli state. In addition an overwhelming record of personal stories of Palestinians has been collected by Christians and non-Christians alike. These stories are endless and parallel what the academic record proves. Most troubling of all, these are things we are simply not being told in our churches.

I am convinced that if the prophets of the Old Testament

were to visit Tel Aviv or West Jerusalem today, their words would be harsh and unremitting. Strangely enough, just as in the Bible, their authority would likely go unrecognized, and like Jeremiah, they would be imprisoned by the Israeli defense forces as a security risk.

What are the deepest problems that trouble the modern state of Israel and contradict its claim to biblical nationhood?

An Exclusivist State

A fundamental problem is found in the character of Israel as a state in the first place. Some of the earliest Zionists seemed to have a vision of a nation that would be free and open to all peoples. Ben Gurion, Israel's first prime minister, repeated this often. In 1946, before Israel was founded, he said to British and American leaders:

> We will have to treat our Arabs and other non-Jewish neighbors on the basis of absolute equality as if they were Jews, but make every effort that they should preserve their Arab characteristics, their language, their Arab culture, their Arab religion, their Arab way of life, while making every effort to make all the citizens of the country equal civilly, socially, economically, politically, intellectually and gradually raise the standard of life of everyone, Jew and others.[16]

This promise never materialized. Israel is a nation that excludes non-Jews by design. Imagine if Holland declared that it was a country built exclusively for white, Dutch Protestant Christians. Others could live there, but they could not form political parties, travel freely, receive equal wages, cultivate an independent culture, or have access to the systems of justice and politics like white, Dutch Protestants. We would be outraged. And, as has happened in South Africa, the world would be severe in its judgment.

Israel makes every attempt to place Palestinians on the margins of society.[17] No nationwide Palestinian organizations have been permitted—whether they are political, economic, or cultural. This means that in the government itself, Palestinians (who make up 18 percent of pre-1967 Israel)[18] are not represented fully. Israel's government is much like the Parliament system of Great Britain. Political parties (of which there are many) enlist voters, and coalitions are formed among parties to gain a majority in the Knesset, a 120-seat Parliament. Individuals do not vote for candidates; rather political office is decided through party representation. Here is the point: For many years no nationwide Palestinian political party has been permitted into the system, so Arabs hold only a few Knesset seats.[19] Further, West Bank and Gaza Palestinians do not even possess the right to vote in national elections.

Self-identity has been repressed so that even showing the four colors of the Palestinian flag in art (green, white, black, and red) can lead to arrest. West Bank Palestinians cannot travel, build a house, obtain a job, or dig a well in their back yard without permission.

Essentially Palestinians within Israel's borders cannot enter the main systems of Israeli society. The major labor organizations, political parties, and even the military are all off limits. Only 4 percent of Israeli university students are Arab because all entrance exams must be taken in Hebrew, and there is much admission discrimination. Further, qualifying Arab students often find that their tuition is not waived, and thus they are economically excluded. On the West Bank Arab universities, which are poorly funded, are viewed as politically suspicious. They have been closed down frequently by the military. Further, an Arab university does not even exist within the pre-1967 borders of Israel. This is creating an entire generation of Palestinians who have become a migrant labor force in low-paying sectors of society: construction, agriculture, and public services (e.g., restaurant workers).

Sometimes the subtleties of discrimination are missed by the foreigner. Israel offers special home mortgage benefits for people who have served in the armed services—which includes virtually all Israelis. However, Palestinians are restricted from joining (for obvious reasons), and thus a whole network of financial benefits are denied to them.

Israel also employs a system for identifying and limiting the movements of its people through its licensing of automobiles. License plates are all color coded: yellow for Israelis, white for Gaza, blue for the West Bank, and green for taxis and service vehicles. West Bank licenses also have a letter before the seven numbers which tells the police the city or village the car comes from.[20] If a "West Bank" car is seen in pre-1967 Israel, say, in Tel Aviv, it will be stopped by the police or army. I asked a well-known architect in Ramallah, Saleem Zaru, if he ever takes his kids to Tel Aviv to the zoo. His answer was telling. Even if he had the travel papers, the harassment because of his license plate would be very upsetting to the whole family. We might note, though, that yellow "Israeli" plates may travel anywhere in the country.

Likewise, everyone is required by law to carry an identification card. Once again there is a color code system to tell a soldier immediately with whom he is dealing. A blue card denotes an Israeli Jew (although Israeli Arabs have this color of card, a note on the card says in Hebrew that the person is "Arab"). An orange card indicates that a person is a West Bank Arab. A red card indicates that a person is from Gaza.[21] A green card indicates that a person is an Arab who was once imprisoned.

When Palestinians are stopped on the street by soldiers, their cards are always checked. Each card has a computer number which a soldier reads over a radio to a computer operator. This massive data base has much information about the Palestinian. If the Arab is not carrying a card or leaves it at home, he is automatically given six months in prison. If an orange West Bank card shows up in Jerusalem and the Arab has no written permission, he or she is arrested. A friend of mine from Ramallah went to West Jerusalem to see a dentist. As she walked down the street, off-duty soldiers stopped her and demanded her card "since she looked Arab." Card checking is a regular form of Israeli intimidation.

All who hold orange West Bank cards must get out of Jerusalem by nightfall. The administrator of a Christian school in the West Bank once had to stay the night at a colleague's home in Jerusalem because he missed his ride. At 2:00 A.M. the army arrived and took him away since he possessed the wrong card. He spent five months in a Hebron prison without ever going to court. Then he was expelled from the country for two years. In order to avoid exile to Lebanon, he went to school in Cairo for the duration of the punishment.

These networks of identifying and controlling the Palestinians have led many to draw comparisons between Israel and South Africa.

Citizenship is a telltale sign of membership in any nation. The Law of Return (1950) declares that every Jew in the world has the right to immigrate to Israel and claim automatic citizenship and social privileges.[22] Not only is this a remarkable statement about Israeli life, but it affects others who have lived on the land for centuries, have fled during war, and are eager to return. Even the United Nations has affirmed the rights of these people to go home.[23] Palestinians whose homes are still in Israel, whose families have lived in the land for centuries, are denied reentry. They languish in camps surrounding Israel's borders or on the West Bank while Jewish newcomers occupy their homes.

Any country that de facto excludes a segment of its society from its national benefits on the basis of race can hardly qualify as democratic. This is why on November 10, 1975, the United Nations declared that Zionism should be considered racism. It is a political philosophy that excludes others based on race, history, and creed.[24] Some writers, such as John Davis, have called the treatment of Palestinians a form of apartheid.[25]

Israel's character stands in stark contrast to the biblical model we have studied in the previous chapters. In the Old Testament the place of the resident alien (the non-Israelite) was assured. He was not denied access to the primary forms of national expression: the temple, the justice system, or the military. Therefore Israel's exclusivism must answer the demands of covenant justice so clearly outlined in the Bible.

Stealing Land

Land ownership has been the darkest side of Israeli history since 1948. While it is true that Israelis purchased land on which to build their settlements and cities, still, this barely accounts for the land to which Israel lays claim today. Both Turkish and British administrations respected the "public properties" and open lands around Arab villages. These lands were collectively owned and reserved for village growth and pasturage. Israeli law has defined this land as state property (under the control of "The Jewish National Fund") and may be used only by Jews. Villages are thus denied room to grow. If land is uncultivated, Israel nationalizes it (often after the Arab farmers have been prohibited from entering it). Sometimes it is taken as "a security zone" or as "needed public property." Palestinian claims to land ownership are aggressively fought in court by government attorneys. If modern documentation cannot be shown, the case is lost, since evidence from before the Israeli occupation is rejected. Some deeds date back to the Turkish period, and these are generally refused by the court. Other Arab families simply do not possess modern documentation—especially those families in rural peasant villages. And since 1967, Israeli law has prohibited West Bank Palestinians from registering their land.

The worst cases of land confiscation are found in the Occupied Territories of Gaza and the West Bank. Land is often closed off, the water rights are removed, and then it is declared abandoned and quickly nationalized. In areas where new Israeli settlements have depleted water tables, Arabs have asked for permits for new wells. These are generally denied, leaving the Arab without water.[26] In the Occupied Territories Israeli land records are kept secret so that Palestinians cannot contest them.[27] Since 1967 about 66 percent of the West Bank and 30 percent of Gaza have been taken.[28]

In addition to the confiscation of "public" lands, Israel has witnessed the military occupation of entire villages, the removal of their residents, and the destruction of their homes. Occasionally Israeli settlers move into them. But generally they are blown up and bulldozed. Hundreds and hundreds of villages have suffered this fate. Al Haq, a Palestinian firm of attorneys begun by Jonathan Kuttab of Jerusalem and Raja Shedadeh of Ramallah, specializes in human rights abuses. According to its records, more than five hundred Arab villages have disappeared since 1948.[29]

In late 1992 a stunning book was published as a testimony to this now-destroyed village life. *Lest the Civilized World Forget: The Colonization of Palestine* is a record of 394 of these villages meticulously researched by Jamil Fayez, a Palestinian physician in North Carolina. Following a summary of the "myths" surrounding the disappearance of these villages, Fayez goes on to list their names—one at a time—providing a sort of litany for the dead.[30] Typical records read like this:

> **57. AL KHAESAH** located 24.8 miles NNE of Safad. Population: 1,840. Obliterated in 1948, with the Jewish settlement of QIRYAT SHEMONA built on its 2,820 acres.

> **107. AL RAMLAH** located 12.5 miles SE of Jaffa. Population: 16,380. Occupied in 1948. Most of its inhabitants were forcefully evicted, while a few hundred remained. The town, renamed RAMLA, was taken over by Jewish immigrants who stole and occupied the houses of the Palestinians. In time they confiscated an additional 442 acres of surrounding lands and gardens.

> **244. IKRET** located NE of Acre near the Lebanese border. Population of 500 Palestinians, all Maronite Christians, who were forced to evacuate their village in 1948. All the village buildings were blown up on Christmas day, 1952, and all its 6,181 acres were stolen.

These three stories are just a sample from the pages and pages that fill the book and help explain why there are 2,500,000 Palestinian refugees in the world. The list reminds me of the Israeli shrine for the Holocaust, Yad Vashem, near Mount Herzel in West Jerusalem. Here records are kept for destroyed Jewish villages in places like Poland. The litany is the same. And yet it seems that no one has learned from history.

The Bible is crystal clear about theft and in particular about the theft of land. The prophets were swift to pronounce judgment on governments that practiced national theft. Those who own land—be they Jew or Gentile—must have their rights protected, or the occupier will find God to be his opponent.

Injustice

Perhaps the most troubling and the most obvious example of injustice is that Israel is holding 1.3 million people captive. This is the population of the West Bank and the Gaza Strip. Much like the "townships" of South Africa, the residents of these places have severe restrictions on their freedoms of speech, movement, and political expression. For example, in 1975 Israel permitted towns such as Nablus, Hebron, Ramallah, and Bethlehem to elect their own mayors. But because these popular leaders supported the Palestine Liberation Organization (PLO), they were deposed, and some were deported.[31]

Israel captured these areas in 1967 but has not dealt with the problem of their populations and has not let them choose their own leaders through elections. Arab villages pay taxes which finance the occupation armies and do not bring the social services Israeli towns enjoy. One village outside Bethlehem (Beit Sahour) refused to pay its taxes, arguing, as a man there told me, "It is the American principle. No taxation without representation." The village of Beit Sahour has suffered severely for the tax rebellion but has been visited and honored by Desmond Tutu and Jimmy Carter for its peaceful efforts.

What will the future hold for these people? Most argue that one of three things must happen: (1) set them free to form their own free state, (2) include them as full citizens in Israel, or (3) incorporate them into Jordan. At least they cannot continue as prisoners of Israel's occupation of 1967.

But each of these options entails tremendous problems:

1. If an independent Palestinian state were built, what guarantees would Israel have that such a nation would not be belligerent? Israel cannot afford to fight a war with armies massed in the mountains all around it. With the rise of Islamic fundamentalism, some Israelis are convinced that such a state would not be moderate at all.

2. Can Israel make the Palestinians full citizens? If Israel makes all Palestinians within its present borders citizens, the Palestinian population will make up 38 percent of the population. Since the birth rate among Palestinians is almost double that of Israelis, in twenty years the Palestinians will make up a majority. Yet some l⸺ at "incorporation" into a larger Israel wouldn't matter anyway. Besides, argue some Arabs, Israel is a *Jewish* state and cannot be genuinely ethnically inclusive.

3. While placing the Palestinians under Jordanian rule would at least place them in an Arab state, still, most

Palestinians have rejected this notion, instead looking for their own national autonomy.

Variations of these three are everywhere. Some speak of a demilitarized West Bank in which Palestinians run the government but cannot have arms. But is this independence? Others speak of "stages of Israeli withdrawal," but doubters look at the countless West Bank settlements and wonder who would have the courage to close them down.

And so while peace conferences continue, these people languish without hope. Around Jerusalem and across the Occupied Territories, Arabs watch in vain as new Israeli settlements are built weekly, securing Israel's grip on the land. This gives the Arabs a feeling of despair and fuels the flames of radicalism.

Oppression and Violence

As discussed in detail above (pp. 109–10), one of the most obvious forms of oppression is that every West Bank and Gaza Palestinian must carry an identification card that tells his or her home, race, and religion. It limits travel, permits the person to hold a job, and records if the military deems him or her a "risk." To be caught without a card means automatic arrest and six months' imprisonment. Soldiers often stop Palestinian youth, examine their cards, and then threaten to keep them unless they do whatever chore the soldiers wish.

Free speech is unheard of among these Palestinians. Arab newspapers published in Jerusalem are strictly censored by the Israeli military authorities. Even some papers published in other countries are illegal in Ramallah and Hebron. Assembling for political demonstrations or free speech is strictly forbidden. Thus these Palestinians have implemented underground communications that impress even the army. Mimeographed fliers telling the news and planning resistance are distributed by children at night. Repression of freedom has been the fuel of the Intifada, whereby Palestinians demand what they have been denied.

Punishment is given in the Occupied Territories, not via a system of civil justice, but through the army. Palestinians do not have recourse to a civil trial, a jury, or the court system enjoyed by others. Security investigations by the army are kept secret so that young men are often punished without knowing the precise nature of their crimes. The army is well known for pursuing corporate punishment and retribution. Villages that sympathize with Palestinian causes may have a number of homes blown up without court jurisdiction. Families with politically active sons and daughters may have their homes demolished without trial. This sort of collective punishment is illegal throughout the Western world.

Even Israeli citizenship is not enough to protect most Palestinians. Riah Abu El Assal is the pastor of the Anglican Church in Nazareth and an Israeli citizen. He once was a candidate for a seat in the Knesset. Yet because as a Christian he felt compelled to speak out about justice, he was placed in "internal exile" in Israel. His passport removed, he could not leave the country or visit the Occupied Territories for three years. El Assal was never given a trial. He never had a chance to defend himself in court.

One of the most distressing studies I have seen was published in 1988 by Al Haq (in Ramallah), a Palestinian human rights organization. It is called *Punishing a Nation: Human Rights Violations During the Palestinian Uprising, December 1987 to December 1988.*[32] The volume itemizes Israel's record of abuse and torture among the Palestinians both in and outside of prison. In the streets the army fires so-called "rubber bullets" at youths throwing stones. These rubber-coated steel balls frequently maim. Concentrated, toxic tear gas is used, which is illegal in the United States. Its repeated use in alleys and buildings has killed many and led countless mothers to miscarry their unborn children. I traveled with a British eye surgeon once who showed me the results of soldiers hitting children across the temple with their clubs. Their aim was so good that they often caused blindness by forcing the children's eyes to virtually pop out. Each child had such similar symptoms that he concluded it must be the result of the soldiers' training.

Let us look at a case study. In 1980 sixteen-year-old Tariq Shumali was accused of throwing a stone at an Israeli vehicle near his home in Beit Sahur. He was beaten so badly that he had to be hospitalized for internal kidney hemorrhaging. No other family members had done anything wrong, nor was anyone given a trial or defense. Yet the boy's father was jailed, his sister was fired from her job as a teacher, the family home was sealed off by soldiers, and the family was deported to an abandoned refugee camp in Jericho, where they lived in a mud-brick hut. The army wanted to make the family an example to the rest of the town.[33]

Time magazine, in its August 31, 1992, issue printed a report of Israeli undercover violence on the West Bank.[34] Military commandos (special units called *sayarot*) dressed like Palestinians infiltrate village homes and assassinate Arab activists. In August Munir Jaradat, age eighteen, was found in the village of Silat al Harithiya and accused of belonging to "the Red Eagles," a violent Palestinian organization. There was no arrest, no trial. Munir was shot dead on the spot.

Leading Israeli legislators have been outraged by these death squads. Israeli Education Minister Shulamit Aloni said she was opposed "to 18 and 19 year old boys [in the army] passing judgment on Palestinians and then carrying out death sentences against them."[35] B'Tselem, an Israeli human rights group, says that only half of the Arabs killed by the commandos are even armed. In one well-publicized incident, Rashid Ghanim, twenty-three, was playing soccer near his home. Four commandos rushed him and shot the unarmed man in cold blood.

Israeli prison camps are notorious for torture. Some camps, such as Ansar, are located in a military compound in the southern desert and are therefore "off limits" to outsiders "for security reasons." Stories from Ansar, the most dreaded of the camps, make depressing reading as people are tortured in unimaginable ways. Cramped, sewage-filled cells, wet bags tied over the head for days, beatings, shock, exposure to sun and scorpions—these are just a few of the recorded incidents. Even pastors of the prisoners are not permitted to visit them.

Because the conflict in the Occupied Territories generally includes minors under eighteen who have thrown stones at soldiers, Israel has earned a reputation for violence to children. According to the Palestine Human Rights Information Center in Jerusalem, Israel has killed one Palestinian child under the age of sixteen an average of every eight days for the past five years.[36] In 1992 a Gaza mental health survey was conducted to measure the results of violence-related trauma to children: Out of an estimated 150,000 children (aged eight to fifteen) in Gaza, more than 63,000 had been beaten by soldiers, 7000 had suffered fractures from those beatings, 35,000 had been struck with some form of Israeli military ammunition, and more than 130,000 had suffered the effects of toxic tear gas five times more concentrated than any tear gas used in the United States.[37]

Numbers like this must be placed in perspective. If the same ratios were applied to the United States (where 53 percent of the population is under age seventeen), the following statistics would result: Over five years, 5,460,000 of the youth would be shot at, beaten, or teargassed by foreign soldiers. It is a staggering scenario. Case studies are in such abundance from every source that few deny them any more. Even Israeli peace organizations such as B'Tselem (which won the Carter Center award for human rights work) has reported astonishing records of abuse.

Take one horrific case published by the Swedish Save the Children Fund. It is summarized by J. A. Graff, whose Canadian publication, *Palestinian Children and Israeli State Violence*, chronicles 138 case studies of military violence to children.

On February 10, 1989, [four-year-old] Ali aimed his toy gun and made clicking noises at a passing Israeli patrol. He was playing near his house in Jabalya refugee camp (Gaza). Seeing this, three soliders raced over. One grabbed the toy and stomped on it, and then grabbed Ali's right hand as another solider held the child from behind. The third soldier "began to pound Ali's outstretched arm with his wooden truncheon. The soldier holding Ali's arm out slapped him hard across the face over and over again." Neighbors tried to intervene but were prevented by the rest of the patrol. The soldiers "continued slapping his face and pounding his arm with the truncheon until the arm broke." Then another soldier "lifted Ali high into the air and dashed him to the pavement. Just as he hit the ground, the soldier who had been slapping his face struck him on the left shoulder with the butt of his rifle. . . . When the three soldiers finished with Ali, they rejoined the patrol and continued down the street."[38]

I have interviewed victims, I have read innumerable first-person reports, I have talked with pastors whose teenagers have been arrested and tortured without reason, and I have witnessed unprovoked violence myself in Israel. It is no wonder that the cycle of violence continues in this land. The biblical prophets would not be amused.

Religious Compromise

I had always entertained the notion that Israel was a very religious place, a place of prayer, of worship, of devotion. On the morning of May 14, 1948, the authors of Israel's Declaration of Independence found themselves debating whether or not to include any reference to God. Ben Gurion decided on ". . . trust in the Rock of Israel" in order to keep from offending anyone.[39] I found this to be remarkable. If indeed this was a nation claiming some continuity with its biblical heritage, surely a reference to God would be acceptable.

Israel functions like a secular state where biblical allusions are used to define and clarify national history. Ultraconservative Jews do live there, but they by no means make up the majority. Jewishness has to do with culture, not necessarily with personal spiritual devotion. As one Israeli leader told me in 1992, less than 30 percent of Israelis are actually practicing their religion. Thus the state recognizes citizenship applications of Jews even if they claim to be atheists. Atheism does not invalidate one's Judaism.[40]

This is a legitimate observation because, as we have seen, possession of the land is tied to obedience to the covenant. God's people cannot make a religious claim to the land without exhibiting religious devotion to the covenant. I am not talking here about the reconstruction of the temple and the revival of its sacrificial ceremonies. I am describing a quality of spirituality, a deep interpretation of life and God's relation to national history. A secular outlook has taken over Israel, and many of us would be hard pressed to distinguish this nation from another secular state.

WHAT WE ARE NOT BEING TOLD

Sadly we are not being told about the relationship between modern-day Israel and the land. We are not being told that Israel is taking land in spite of the just complaints of the families living on the land. Israel is committing the sin of Ahab.

Christian pastors throughout the Middle East are trying to be heard. Naim Ateek (whose story about Beisan was told in chapter 4) is a responsible Christian leader whose pain runs deep. Stories such as his are extremely common today. Other Palestinian Christian pastors have told their stories as well, and some have suffered significantly for speaking out. For example, Elias Chacour, a pastor in Galilee, also lost his childhood home in 1948 when Israeli troops evacuated and destroyed his father's village of Biram. The Israelis were "depopulating" that area as well.[41] Audi Rantisi is another pastor who now serves in Ramallah. His home was in Lydda, and the Israelis coveted his family's land and removed all of his Palestinian Christian neighbors at gunpoint.[42] He grew up in a tent city outside of Ramallah.

These are credible men whose voices are just now being heard as evangelical publishers have published their stories. They are courageous men of God whose anguished reports deserve an audience. Every refugee camp in Israel is filled with stories of families who fled and then found new barbed wire keeping them from going home.

But perhaps the stories of individual villages like Beisan are most compelling. Ibiliin, the village parish of Father Elias Chacour, is nestled in the rolling hills of Galilee near Nazareth. It is a peaceful place with good soil, good rainfall, and no record of anti-Israeli conflict. Yet as of 1989 the Israeli government has illegally confiscated as much as 70 percent of Ibiliin's lands.[43]

As evangelicals we need to take a closer look at the character of Israel. If Israel's appeal to nationhood, to possessing the land, is buttressed by an appeal to biblical promise, then its record of national life must be open to inspection. If this is the basis of Israeli nationhood, then modern Israel must be judged by the standards that the prophets applied to biblical Israel. Today Palestinian Christian leaders in the land, Christian relief agencies (evangelical and mainline), and secular agencies (such as the Red Cross, the United Nations, and Amnesty International) all offer the same complaint: Israel is not promoting justice.

The very Scriptures in which Israel has anchored its hope are the Scriptures that judge Israel today. Jesus was outraged by the complacency and belligerence of Jewish leaders who condemned him. They appealed to their Scriptures to justify their privileged position as God's people to reject what God was saying to them through Jesus. "Do not think that I shall accuse you to the Father; it is Moses who accuses you, on whom you set your hope" (John 5:45). The Bible that bears the promises of God likewise bears the expectations of God. And when these expectations are ignored, when righteousness is thrown to the winds, the prophetic voice cannot be silenced: God's displeasure will be stirred and his judgment will be swift.

NOTES

1. New York: Putnam, 1975.
2. Tel Aviv: n.p., 1965.
3. See also R. Slater, *Golda. The Uncrowned Queen of Israel. A Pictorial Biography* (New York: Jonathan David, 1981). Another fascinating story of personal experiences, though written with a much harsher tone, is that of Menachem Begin (Israel's sixth prime minister, 1977–83): *The Revolt* (Los Angeles: Nash, 1972). This is Begin's account published originally in 1948, describing events leading up to the birth of modern Israel.
4. Golda Meir's birth name was Goldie Mabovitch. After her marriage, she became Goldie Myerson, and in 1956 she Hebraized her name to Golda Meir.
5. Before the war of 1948, Golda Meir negotiated extensively with King Abdullah of Jordan, trying to keep his country neutral before the upcoming war. In this capacity she traveled in disguise to Jordan wearing Arab dress and accompanied by an unarmed translator. Abdullah had never negotiated face to face with an Israeli like Meir. In fact, he had never met a woman diplomat in the Middle East before!

Courage, cleverness, and unyielding debate were typical of this remarkable woman.

6. T. L. Friedman, *From Beirut to Jerusalem* (New York: Doubleday, 1989). Friedman has been the recipient of numerous awards in journalism. Today he lives in Washington, D.C., and works as the *New York Times* chief diplomatic correspondent covering the State Department and foreign affairs.

7. Ibid., 4.

8. Ibid., 284.

9. But we must be clear that in no way were the earliest Zionists "religious." The biblical traditions were mere metaphors. The "New Israeli" or "New Jew," as they called these early pioneers, was a secular, cultural Jew.

10. William Blackstone, "May the United States Intercede for the Jews?" *Our Day* 8 (October 1898): 46.

11. London: Marshall, Morgan & Scott, 1958.

12. Walvoord's three earliest books are *Israel in Prophecy* (1962), *The Church in Prophecy* (1964), and *The Nations in Prophecy* (1967). These are currently bound together as *The Nations, Israel and the Church in Prophecy* (Grand Rapids: Zondervan, 1988). Similarly see W. M. Smith, *Israeli/Arab Conflict and the Bible* (Glendale: Regal/Gospel Light, 1967).

13. H. Lindsey (with C. C. Carlson), *The Late Great Planet Earth* (Grand Rapids: Zondervan, 1970). See also the excellent critique of T. Boersma, *Is the Bible a Jigsaw Puzzle? An Evaluation of Hal Lindsey's Writings* (St. Catherine's, Ont.: Paideia Press, 1978).

14. H. Lindsey, *The 1980s: Countdown to Armageddon* (New York: Bantam, 1981).

15. *Late Great Planet Earth*, 58.

16. *The Jewish Case: Before the Anglo-American Committee of Inquiry on Palestine as Presented by the Jewish Agency for Palestine* (Jerusalem: Jewish Agency for Palestine, 1947), 71, as cited in R. and H. Ruether, *Wrath of Jonah. The Crisis of Religious Nationalism in the Israeli-Palestinian Conflict* (New York: Harper & Row, 1989), 132, n. 5.

17. See the comprehensive studies of I. Lustick, *Arabs in the Jewish State: Israel's Control of a National Minority* (Austin, Tex.: Univ. of Texas Press, 1980).

18. I am using the following population figures for Israel/-Palestine: In pre-1967 borders, the Jewish population is 3.5 million; the Palestinian population is 800,000. The West Bank and Gaza have 1.3 million Palestinians. See the statistics and their sources in N. Ateek, *Justice and Only Justice* (Maryknoll, N.Y.: Orbis, 1989), 3–5.

19. Nazih Qurah, "The Arabs in Israel Since 1948," *Zionism and Racism* (Tripoli: n.p., 1977), 94–96.

20. For instance, Hebrew R [resh] on white background is Ramallah, H is Hebron, B is Bethlehem. A yellow background indicates a village near these towns: a yellow R is a village near Ramallah, etc.

21. This card was dark green prior to the Intifada.

22. Jewishness, though, has been carefully defined by Israel's Orthodox rabbis. They exclude illegitimate children of Jewish parents, children with a Jewish father but whose mother became a Christian, and Jewish believers in Jesus. A number of others are excluded as well, such as converts to Reformed or Conservative Judaism. Technically, a Jewish person who was an atheist would qualify as a Jew and be able to claim citizenship. See S. Z. Abramov, "Who Is a Jew?" in S. Z. Abramov, *Perpetual Dilemma. Jewish Religion in the Jewish State* (Cranbury, N.J.: Associated Univ. Press, 1976), 270–320.

23. United Nations General Resolution #194, December 11, 1948.

24. United Nations Resolution #3379 (November 10, 1975). The full text and background can be found in *Zionism and Racism, Proceedings of an International Symposium* (Tripoli: n.p., 1977). The United Nations, under strong pressure from the United States, removed this decision in 1991.

25. J. H. Davis, *The Evasive Peace* (New York: New World Press, 1968), 115. Davis worked for many years in the Middle East with the United Nations Relief & Works Agency (UNRWA). See also Uri Davis, *Israel: An Apartheid State* (London: Zed Books, 1987).

26. From 1967 to 1983 only five permits for new wells were granted to Palestinians. Raja Shehadeh, *Occupier's Law: Israel and the West Bank* (Washington, D.C.: Institute for Palestinian Studies, 1985), 153–54.

27. Ibid., 39–40, as cited in R. and H. Ruether, *Wrath of Jonah,* 156, n. 55.

28. Personal interview, Reverend Don Wagner of Mercy Corps, an international Christian human rights ministry based in Chicago.

29. Cf. Israel Shahak, "Arab Villages Destroyed in Israel: A Report," in *Documents from Israel* (London: Ithaca Press, 1975), 47; also Sabri Jiryis, *The Arabs in Israel* (New York: Monthly Review Press, 1976).

30. *Lest the Civilized World Forget. The Colonization of Palestine,* published by Americans for Middle East Understanding, 475 Riverside Drive, Room 241, New York, NY 10115. (212)-870-2053; FAX (212)-870-2050.

31. Some were even attacked, but no one knows if the army or Israeli settlers did it. Karim Khalaf, mayor of Ramalah, Basaam Shaka'a, mayor of Nablus, and Ibrahim Tawil, mayor of El Bireh, were all attacked by bombs. Rahad Kawasme, mayor of Hebron, was deported and later assassinated in Jordan. See R. and H. Ruether, *Wrath of Jonah*, 158–59, who conducted personal interviews with these leaders. In spring 1993 many of these leaders were permitted to return after almost twenty years in exile.

32. The volume is carefully organized with well-documented cases of abuses. Chapters include "Use of Torture" (chap. 1), "Obstruction of Medical Treatment" (chap. 2), "Settler Use of Excessive Force" (chap. 3), "Methods of Punishment" (chap. 4), "Curfews" (chap. 5), "The Administration of Justice" (chap. 6), "Economic Sanctions" (chap. 7), "Repression of Education" (chap. 8), "Repression of Organizational Activity" (chap. 9). See also Amnesty International's *Israel and the Occupied Territories. The Military Justice System in the Occupied Territories: Detention, Interrogation and Trial Procedures* (July 1991).

33. C. Chapman, *Whose Promised Land?* (Herts, Eng.: Lion, 1983), 179. Chapman is a Christian minister who has been working with university students in the Middle East since 1968. Stories such as this are commonplace, and there is an abundance of records of them from highly credible sources.

34. "Deadly Force. How Israeli Commandos Are Waging an Undercover War in the Occupied Territories," *Time*, August 31, 1992, 49–50.

35. Ibid.

36. J. A. Graff, "An Open Letter to Mrs. Clinton," *The Link* 26, no. 2 (May–June 1993): 3.

37. Ibid. During the Intifada in December 1987, the United States rushed 150,000 canisters of this banned gas to Israel from a plant in Saltsburg, Pennsylvania.

38. Ibid. Quotations are from the Swedish report. See Graff's full treatment, *Palestinian Children and Israeli State Violence* (Near East Cultural and Education Foundation of Canada, 1991).

39. Golda Meir, *My Life*, 223.

40. Studies of the complex relation between politics and religion in Israel are abundant. See C. S. Liebman and E. Don-Yehiya, *Religion and Politics in Israel* (Bloomington: Univ. Of Indiana Press, 1984); idem., *Civil Religion in Israel. Traditional Judaism and Political Culture in the Jewish State* (Berkeley: Univ. of California Press, 1983); Abramov, *Perpetual Dilemma*.

41. E. Chacour, *Blood Brothers* (Old Tappan, N.J.: Revell, 1984).

42. A Rantisi, *Blessed Are the Peacemakers. A Palestinian Christian in the Occupied West Bank* (Grand Rapids: Zondervan, 1990).

43. E. Chacour, *We Belong to the Land. The Story of a Palestinian Israeli Who Lives for Peace and Reconciliation* (New York: Harper & Row, 1990), 24. Chacour refers to data in Sabri Jiryis, *The Arabs in Israel* (New York: Monthly Review Press, 1976), 295, table 5.

Part Three

Christians and the Land

Chapter Seven

THE NEW TESTAMENT AND THE LAND

"The nation of Israel today is a nation among nations, and
. . . it must be judged as any other political state. But to
identify modern Israel, the state or the Jewish people, with
'the Israel of God' is to miss the teaching of the New
Testament at one of its most vital points." (Frank Stagg,
"The Israel of God in the New Testament," in *Christians,
Zionism, and Palestine*, 65–66)[1]

Jesus said to her, "Woman, believe me, the hour is coming
when you will worship the Father neither on this mountain
nor in Jerusalem. . . . But the hour is coming, and is now
here, when the true worshipers will worship the Father in
spirit and truth, for the Father seeks such as these to
worship him." (John 4:21–23)

After his assistant had served us Arabic coffee, I asked
Father George Makhlouf a question. "How can you argue with
the Israeli claim to own this land since God gave it to the Jews
in the Old Testament? Israeli Jews have inherited the promises
to Abraham, have they not?" Father George (as he is called) is
no stranger to such questions. As parish priest of St. George's
Greek Orthodox Church in Ramallah, he has been fielding
them for years. "The church," he began, "has inherited the
promises of Israel. The church is actually the new Israel. What
Abraham was promised, Christians now possess because they

are Abraham's true spiritual children just as the New Testament teaches."[2]

In Father George's view, what I have written so far would have only marginal value for Christian thought. The New Testament announces a new covenant filled with new promises. It also identifies Christian believers as the true children of Abraham—in other words, they are the heirs of Abraham's original promises. Therefore we are obligated to read the Old Testament through the New Testament, and when we do, suddenly it becomes clear that the church has replaced the nation of Israel.

This way of viewing the problem of Israel/Palestine is called "replacement theology," and its adherents are as vocal and passionate as its critics. But the Greek Orthodox tradition of Father George has been consistent. From the earliest centuries the Middle Eastern churches have claimed the promises of the Old Testament for their own.[3] This shows up even in Orthodox iconography. Churches display beautiful pictures (or icons) of Old Testament stories whose truths have now been swept up by the Christian tradition and "baptized" with new meaning. Father George's sanctuary in the Old Quarter of Ramallah is a case in point.

One of the surprising things about the New Testament is that it never refers to the land promises of Abraham directly. This is peculiar, especially when we recall how many times the Old Testament mentions the theme. Was "land" an interest of Jesus? Did Paul reflect on the nation of Israel and the identity of the church? If Christians are "children of Abraham," do they inherit Abraham's promises?

"THE LAND" AMONG JESUS' CONTEMPORARIES

The first question we must ask is whether or not the people of Israel were talking about the land in Jesus' day, whether they were as interested in the promises of Abraham in this later period as they were in the Old Testament. No scholar has given as much energy to this subject as W. D. Davies of Duke University.[4] Davies makes clear that the rabbis in the New Testament era did indeed have a passionate interest in the "land." Writings from this period refer to "the holy land," frequently describing it as "a goodly land" and "a land which is in thy sight the most precious of all lands." The land of Israel/Palestine is "extensive and beautiful," "pleasant and glorious," and promised for those who are faithful to God.[5] This devotion increased when the people considered how they lived under the heel of the Roman army and were not free to enjoy the bounty of the land as God had planned. In describing the work of the coming Messiah, the first-century Psalms of Solomon says,

> And he shall gather together a holy people . . .
> And he shall divide them according to their tribes
> *upon the land*
> And neither sojourner nor alien shall sojourn with them
> any more.[6]

The rabbis could not separate Israel, God, and the land. Possessing the land of Israel/Palestine was intrinsic to being Jewish. The land was the place of God's revelation and the principal place where God could be known. The volume of oral laws from this period—the Mishna—devotes fully 35 percent of its pages to issues connected with the land. The Mishna acknowledges that even the laws recorded in the Old Testament Scriptures presupposed residence in the land: agricultural tithes applied to produce grown in the land; cities of refuge crucial for civil law could be built only in the land. Listen to the words of the Mishna itself:

> "There are ten degrees of holiness. The Land of Israel is holier than any other land. Wherein lies its holiness? In that from it they may bring [the offerings of] the sheaf, the firstfruits, and the two loaves, which they may not bring from any other land."[7]

The centrality of the land is clear even in the prayers of the Jews in this period. The so-called "Eighteen Benedictions" were recited three times each day as an expression of daily piety. Note how Benedictions 14, 16, and 18 emphasize that devotion to the land of Israel and the city of Jerusalem is necessary for faith.

Benediction 14

Be merciful, O Lord our God, in Thy great mercy towards Israel Thy people, and towards Jerusalem Thy city, and towards Zion, the abiding place of thy glory, and towards Thy temple and Thy habitation, and towards the kingdom of the house of David, Thy righteous anointed one. Blessed art Thou, O Lord God of David, the builder of Jerusalem.

Benediction 16

Accept us, O Lord our God, and dwell in Zion; and may Thy servants serve thee in Jerusalem. Blessed art Thou, O Lord, whom in reverent fear we worship.

Benediction 18

Bestow Thy peace upon Israel Thy people and upon Thy city and upon Thine inheritance, and bless us, all of us together. Blessed art Thou, O Lord, who makes peace.

After Jerusalem was destroyed by Rome in A.D. 70, this devotion increased as writers described longingly the way life had been before the war. The loss of the land in the destruction of Jerusalem was so acute that the event was acknowledged each year by three weeks of fasting which concluded on the ninth of Ab, the fifth month of the Jewish calendar.[8]

JESUS AND THE LAND IN MATTHEW, MARK, AND LUKE

We have to keep this first-century background in mind when we open the Gospels. If Judaism was highly conscious of the place of land for faith, it is all the more surprising that Jesus fails to mention the land in any significant way. The land and the city of Jerusalem are not featured in his teachings. In fact, Jesus does not even revere Jerusalem as did the rabbis of his era. For him, Galilee "of the Gentiles" is a place of faith, while Jerusalem is the city that kills the prophets and the Messiah (Matt. 21:33–41; 23:37–39).[9] Jesus reveals his glory for the first time in Galilee (Mark 1:14–15; John 2:1–11). Following the Crucifixion, the disciples are even directed to go to Galilee to witness the risen Lord (Mark 16:7). In a culture that is keenly devoted to Jerusalem, this is highly unusual. In Jesus' prayers and in his teachings about prayer, he does not include the land of Israel or the city of Jerusalem once.

I am convinced that Jesus was challenging the connection Israel had made between the possession of land and faith in God. Israel had linked political nationhood with covenant blessing, and Jesus stood ready to question their assumptions. In Jesus' teachings, something new was afoot.[10]

Jesus' emphasis on the kingdom of God gave him every opportunity to talk about land and inheritance, but he refused. He would not define the Messiah as one who would remove Israel from Roman rule and build a new nation. After his death his followers despaired that he did not "redeem Israel" (Luke 24:21). Even after Jesus' resurrection, his disciples asked, "Lord, is this the time when you will restore the kingdom to Israel?" (Acts 1:6). Their minds were on political restoration, but for Jesus, God's kingdom was fundamentally God's reign over the lives of men and women—not an empire.[11]

On the one hand, Jesus' words reflect those of the Old Testament prophets when he says that those who possess the land must exhibit righteousness or else they will lose their gift. This is quite clear, for instance, in Mark 12:1–11, where Jesus tells the parable of the vineyard. Thanks to Isaiah, "the vineyard" was a premier metaphor for the land of Israel. In this parable Jesus describes residents of the vineyard who reject and kill God's messengers and God's Son. Then the owner of the vineyard (God) makes a judgment: "What then will the owner of the vineyard do? He will come and destroy the tenants and give the vineyard to others" (Mark 12:9). Matthew's account of the same parable makes the climax even more severe: "He will put those wretches to a miserable death, and lease the vineyard to other tenants who will give him the produce at the harvest time" (Matt. 21:41). It is not surprising that after Jesus gives this conclusion, the Jewish leadership tries to arrest him.[12]

But note that Jesus goes one step beyond the Old Testament prophets. He says that new tenants, new occupants, will gain the vineyard. New residents will come to the land of Israel. In his book *The Land*, Walter Bruggemann finds Jesus' teaching about "reversal" at work here. In the economy of Jesus' kingdom, those who weep shall rejoice, those who want to be first must become last, those who grasp at life will lose it—and those who grasp onto the land as if it were their property will find it going to others.[13] This theme of "inversion" (rich becoming poor, blind gaining sight, proud becoming humble, etc.) is at the heart of Jesus' gospel. "Graspers of land" will suddenly find themselves at a loss.[14] And who shall inherit "the earth"? Not those who demand it, but those who are empty, those who are meek (Matt. 5:5).

It is interesting to reflect on Jesus' own landless condition. In the culture of the Middle East, the possession of land and the claim to heritage through property were crucial values. But Jesus was without land, without home. In Matthew 8:20 Jesus responds to a disciple by saying, "Foxes have holes, and birds of the air have nests; but the Son of Man has nowhere to lay his head." Landlessness is a part of Jesus' own life. Nowhere does Jesus promise that the possession of land is a by-product of membership in his kingdom.

JESUS AND THE TRUE ISRAEL

Jesus' criticism of the theological status quo in Judaism can be seen in yet one more way. Not only did he reject those who would strive after the material benefits of their faith (e.g., land), but he also announced that his kingdom was inaugurating a new people of God. Jesus uprooted the assumption that the benefits of land permanently came to Israel. Now he says that these benefits come to someone else, men and women living in concert with his dawning kingdom.

Jesus did not come to start a new movement outside of Judaism. He did not wish to compete with Judaism. He came in full submission to Jewish faith: he obeyed the law, observed the festivals, and respected temple worship. He was an Israelite par excellence. However, Israel rejected both Jesus and his kingdom, and as a result, he predicted judgment on the land and the scattering of Israel. "The Jewish nation which rejected the offer of the Kingdom of God [was] therefore set aside as the people of God and is to be replaced by a new people."[15]

Initially these new people were not Gentiles, however. They were Jews who responded in faith and formed the nucleus of Jesus' earliest followers. This was God's plan for Israel: those who accepted the Messiah became the new Israel. "Jesus' disciples are . . . the people of the Kingdom, the true Israel."[16] This is why the Gospels are filled with so much imagery from Israel's nationhood: Jesus is a new Moses, he inaugurates a new exodus, and his twelve apostles symbolize the twelve tribes. His new covenant stands in contrast to the covenant of Sinai.[17]

Did God therefore reject his people, the descendants of Abraham, Isaac, and Jacob? Not at all! The concept that explains this notion of Jesus' disciples as the true Israel in continuity with Judaism comes from the Old Testament theme of "the believing remnant." During times of faithlessness in Israel's history, God had a "faithful remnant" of people who did not fall away. These believers who did not succumb to Canaanite or Egyptian religion were "the true Israel."[18]

Jesus' followers, therefore, represent Israel's remnant. They are at the center of God's new effort in the world. And if this is the case, they are heirs to the promises God has always extended to his faithful followers.

JESUS AND THE LAND IN THE GOSPEL OF JOHN

If Matthew, Mark, and Luke show us teachings of Jesus that challenge the security of holding on to land in Jewish religion, John introduces us to yet another approach to the question. In this gospel Jesus spiritualizes the promise of land. But here we have to be careful with our language. Jesus does not devalue "the material world" as if only spiritual realities were important.[19] This would deny the world itself which God created—to which Jesus in the flesh belongs. In this gospel, Jesus takes a different view: Jesus himself becomes the locus of holy space. The aim of the old covenant was the land of promise; now the aim is Jesus Christ, who walked in the land.

This teaching is made clear in all of the passages where Jesus is compared with the religious benefits of the land. For example, the temple in Jerusalem is found to be lacking in comparison with Jesus, whose body itself is "a temple" (2:21–22). Holy places like Bethel (where Jacob saw his vision) are surpassed by this Jesus upon whom "angels of God ascend and descend" (1:51). Jacob's well in Samaria offers no drink like Jesus' living water (4:10). The pool at Bethesda in Jerusalem cannot compare with Jesus, the one who truly heals (5:1–9). Sacred sites now fade in comparison with Jesus, who offers what the site only suggests.

Perhaps the most important example of this change is found in Jesus' conversation with the Samaritan woman. When she points to her "holy mountain" (Mount Gerizim) and compares it with Jerusalem (another Jewish "holy mountain"), Jesus negates both: "Woman, believe me, the hour is coming when you will worship the Father neither on this mountain nor in Jerusalem. . . . But the hour is coming, and is now here, when the true worshipers will worship the Father in spirit and truth, for the Father seeks such as these to worship him" (John 4:21–23). The most holy place of all, Jerusalem, is set aside for true worship generated by the Spirit. Jesus is redefining the place of promise where God will meet his people.

The drama of salvation in the Old Testament centers around the acquisition and the keeping of Abraham's land of promise. Curiously, this promise of a place, a home, is echoed in Jesus' words in John 14. Jesus goes ahead of us "to prepare a place for us." And he explains that this place will be among the many "rooms" (Gk. *mone*) in his Father's house. This word *room* was commonly used in Judaism to refer to the place of promise, namely the land of Israel. In John 14, however, the "place" is defined again and again until we learn that it is actually the indwelling of Father, Son, and Spirit in the believer's life: "we will come to him and make our home [*mone*] with him" (14:23). Once again, Jesus is pointing to a higher gift, a different promise, which fulfills and replaces the need for land.

We have already learned how the vineyard was a prominent symbol for the land of Israel. In the fourth gospel it appears in a unique passage in chapter 15. Here residence in the vineyard is measured by one thing: Are we connected to the Vine? Are we bearing fruit? Jesus says, "I am the true vine" not "Israel is the true vineyard." Therefore valid connection with the vineyard must be made through him.

John's contribution is quite simple. Jesus is a new Moses

(1:17) who can even duplicate and surpass Moses' feeding miracle of the wilderness (6:1–34). Just as Moses was leading the people of Israel to their promised land, so too, Jesus leads God's people. But now we learn that Jesus himself is in reality that which the land had offered only in form. To grasp after land is like grasping after bread—when all along we should discover that Jesus is "the bread of life" (6:35).

Putting it in more technical terms, John translates the promise of land and place into the reality of Jesus. To use the words of W. D. Davies, John shows Jesus displacing holy space.[20] John "christifies" holy space.[21] Christ is the reality behind all earthbound promises. When John writes that "we beheld his glory," he is attributing the glory of God to the presence of Jesus, a glory that could be found only in the land. When John says that "the word became flesh and dwelt among us" he uses a special term: *dwelt* is the same word for tabernacle throughout the Old Testament.[22] In effect, Jesus is the new place of God's dwelling.

To sum up, we might observe a cycle of responses to the question of land: (1) land is rejected as the aim of faith; (2) land is *spiritualized* as meaning something else; (3) the new promise is *historicized* in Jesus, a man who lives in the land; (4) the promise is *sacramentalized*—that is, as a sacrament bears testimony to things beyond what we see and touch (without denying these properties), so too Jesus' "landness" (his physicality) is a reality, but believers are urged to push further, to find the "living water" and "bread of life" that he offers.[23]

THE EARLIEST CHRISTIANS

The potent biblical metaphor of land was not lost on the earliest Christians. They realized that in Christ the promises of the Old Testament had now been extended to them. They began to live out what Christ had announced: Followers of Jesus were the new people of God. And they would inherit the history and the promises known throughout the Old Testament.

The use of the land metaphor for discipleship in Hebrews 3–4 makes this most clear. In these chapters the Christian walk is compared with Moses and Joshua leading Israel through the wilderness. For them, the promised rest was the land of Canaan. Hebrews now uses this story to describe the "promised rest" extended to Christians. Land is spiritualized, to be sure, but it is interesting that the writer of this book employed such a powerful Jewish theme. Whatever the "land" meant in the Old Testament, whatever the promise contained, this now belonged to Christians. Hence, a "central symbol for the promise of the gospel is land."[24]

Perhaps the most dramatic redefinition of "land" is found in Hebrews 11. Echoing the story of Genesis, this chapter reminds us how Abraham was called to depart from his homeland in order to inherit a new land God had promised. Hebrews 11:8 makes it clear that this is a reference to the land of Israel/Palestine (known then as Canaan). *But remarkably we learn that this land was not really the place of God's promise.* The land was a metaphor, a symbol of a greater place beyond the soil of Canaan.

> By faith he [Abraham] stayed for a time in the land he had been promised, as in a foreign land, living in tents, as did Isaac and Jacob, who were heirs with him of the same promise. For he looked forward to the city that has foundations, whose architect and builder is God. (Heb. 11:9–10)

As we know, Abraham settled in the promised land, and God's promise to him was seemingly fulfilled. But then we read in 11:13 just the opposite! "All of these died in faith *without having received the promises,* but from a distance they saw and greeted them." (*Emphasis mine.*) Abraham's *true promise* was not the physical land, but a higher promise that went beyond mere land. The book of Hebrews says that Abraham and his descendants

> confessed that they were strangers and foreigners on the earth, for people who speak in this way make it clear that they are seeking a homeland. If they had been thinking of the land that they had left behind, they would have had opportunity to return. But as it is, they desire a better country, that is, a heavenly one. Therefore God is not

ashamed to be called their God; indeed, he has prepared a
city for them. (Heb. 11:14–16)

Therefore Hebrews tells us that God's intentions went far
beyond the land. The "city" God has prepared for them is not
Jerusalem. We might say that in this passage the land is being
spiritualized, viewed as a vehicle to something else. The
promise to Abraham is actually fulfilled in heaven.

No doubt the entry of Greek-speaking Jews into the church
gave early Christianity a unique perspective on land. So-called
"Hellenistic Jews" were open to the larger Mediterranean
world. They did not speak only Hebrew. In fact, some had lost
Hebrew altogether and could speak only Greek! And few were
willing to view Israel/Palestine as the only place of residence
appropriate for a Jew. They did not adhere to the Jewish
nationalism of the day and were quick to be free of it. Stephen
was one of the Hellenistic Jews who embraced faith in Christ in
Jerusalem. In Acts 7 he gives one of the longest speeches in the
book of Acts, clearly defending his "openness" against harsh
criticisms from Jewish leadership. What Stephen says in this
speech is important. He outlines how God had spoken in other
foreign lands, such as Mesopotamia (Abraham) and Egypt
(Joseph, Moses). From this he concludes that God's work is not
limited to the land of Israel/Palestine alone. God is not confined
to the geography of Israel's land. Stephen challenges the Jewish
assumption that the land is integral to the plan of God. He
critiques the wedding of nation and religion that had run
rampant in first-century Judaism and fueled hostilities not just
with Rome, but with any believer who refused to put land at
the center of his or her faith.

In fact, it was Stephen's wisdom, his creative openness,
that led the early church to cross the cultural boundaries
erected in that day. Mission could now go forward to Samaria,
to Gentiles in Caesarea, and to the rest of the world. The land
of Israel/Palestine did not exhaust God's agenda for humanity.

THE LAND IN THE WRITINGS OF PAUL

Paul likewise probed the historic continuity between Israel
itself and the church. Since the earliest Christians were Jews,

they easily viewed themselves as heirs of Abraham's promises. But then the troubling question arose: had the church completely replaced Israel as the people of God? Was Judaism without Christ still esteemed in God's eyes? Did these Jews still possess any of the promises of Abraham?

While Paul does not refer to the patriarchal promises and the land directly, his exhaustive rabbinic training equipped him to think in metaphors that were commonplace in Judaism. For him, there is genuine continuity between the people of God in the Old Testament and the people of God in the New Testament. Christians are now "the children of Abraham." Qualifying is not a matter of ritual or bloodline.[25]

This is exactly the argument of Paul in Romans 2:25–29. Religious ritual or heritage does not determine spiritual privileges: "A person is a Jew who is one inwardly, and real circumcision is a matter of the heart—it is spiritual and not literal" (2:29). For Paul, this opens the way for Gentiles to stand before God with Jews and have equal status. The key determinant is faith in Christ.

In Galatians 3–4 and Romans 4 Paul emphasizes Abraham as a model for faith and finds in the patriarch the ancestor of Christians who also by faith find righteousness. Therefore there is a link: Abraham was a man of faith, and his children are those who exhibit a parallel faith.

The next step is important. If believing Christians are indeed children of Abraham through faith, then they are also Abraham's heirs. Listen to Paul's words directly:

> "For the promise that he would inherit the world did not come to Abraham or to his descendants through the law but through the righteousness of faith. If it is the adherents of the law who are to be the heirs, faith is null and the promise is void." (Rom. 4:13–14)

> ". . . and if [we are] children, then heirs, heirs of God and joint heirs with Christ—if, in fact, we suffer with him so that we may also be glorified with him." (Rom. 8:17)

> ". . . that in Christ Jesus the blessing of Abraham might come to the Gentiles, so that we might receive the promise of the Spirit through faith. . . . For if the inheritance comes

from the law, it no longer comes from the promise; but God
granted it to Abraham through the promise." (Gal. 3:14, 18)

Paul thus sees Christians as receiving Abraham's promises. And "land" is among those promises! Bruggemann
comments: "It is central to Paul's argument that the promise
endures. The heirs in Christ are not heirs to a new promise, but
the one which abides, and that is centrally land."[26] In Galatians
3:15–18 Paul makes a very subtle, but very important, suggestion. The ancient promises were made, he says, to Abraham
and to "his offspring." Using a style of rabbinic argument less
familiar to us today, Paul stresses that "offspring" is singular,
not plural: "It does not say, 'And to offsprings,' as of many; but
it says, 'And to your offspring,' that is, to one person, who is
Christ" (Gal. 3:16). Hence, Christ is the recipient of Abraham's
blessings, and if we are "in Christ," we are heirs both of Christ
and of Abraham simultaneously. Christ is thus "the Seed of
Abraham par excellence and all who are in him are equally
Abraham's sons."[27]

This continuity between Abraham and the church must
have been important. It explains why at the end of Galatians
Paul may refer to the church as "Israel" ("As for those who will
follow this rule—peace be upon them, and mercy, and upon
the Israel of God" 6:16).[28] In Ephesians 2:11–22 he wants to
describe Gentiles as enjoying the blessings of "those who are
near." Judaism has no privileges that exclude Gentiles since the
coming of Christ. God's aim is to "make one new person"
instead of the two. "Jew" and "Gentile" are no longer useful
categories. Now there is only one category: the believer in
Christ.

Other writers made the same point. Peter, for instance,
writes his first letter to Christians who live throughout the
Mediterranean world (1 Peter 1:1). But then he addresses these
Christians using language taken directly from the Old Testament for Israel:

> But you are a chosen race, a royal priesthood, a holy nation,
> God's own people, in order that you may proclaim the
> mighty acts of him who called you out of darkness into his
> marvelous light.

> Once you were not a people,
>   but now you are God's people;
> once you had not received mercy,
>   but now you have received mercy. (1 Peter 2:9–10)

Clearly these verses draw on titles from the book of Exodus (19:6; 23:22). They are a conscious attempt to designate the church as a new people of God.[29] As Peter Richardson writes, "The Church has taken over the inheritance of Israel (1 Peter 1:4)."[30] James does the same thing when he refers to the church as "the twelve tribes [of Israel]" (James 1:1).[31]

ROMANS 9–11, PAUL'S PROVISION FOR ISRAEL

If the church has indeed become the people of God, the new Israel, what happens to Israel "outside of Christ"? Paul explains his view of unbelieving Israel in Romans 9–11. These chapters are critical for us since this is the one place where the church and Israel are contrasted directly.

First, Paul affirms that God has not rejected Israel, because he himself is an Israelite and so are other Jewish Christians like him. Drawing again on the Old Testament notion of a remnant, Paul argues that Christian believers are the new remnant in God's working: "So too at the present time there is a remnant, chosen by grace" (Rom. 11:5).[32] Thus in 11:1 when Paul thinks about the question, "Has God rejected his people?" he replies emphatically, "By no means!" The key is in 11:2, "God has not rejected his people whom he foreknew." The remnant is the body of believers within Israel who have kept faith with the covenant and God's purposes. And God knows who they are. Therefore God has been faithful to his covenant people because these people are found now within the church. Israel in Christ is now heir to the great covenant history of the Old Testament.[33]

Is this remnant simply Jewish Christians? Not at all. In 9:25–26 Paul cites Hosea's referring to Gentiles: "And in the very place where it was said to them, 'You are not my people,' *there*[34] they shall be called children of the living God." (*Emphasis mine.*) Where was this proclamation given? Jerusalem. God's holy city is the place where the church—filled with Jews and Gentiles—as the remnant, the body of believers predicted by Hosea, will be announced fulfilling God's purposes.

Second, Paul develops the picture of an olive tree as an image of God's people in history. It has many branches and thus, many people. Paul says that unbelieving Israel is like a branch broken off from the trunk of this tree.[35] That is, unbelieving Israel has been rejected (11:15) and "broken off" (11:20) so that gentile believers might be "grafted in" (11:17–19). "God's people" (the tree trunk) is a wider concept than just Israel alone. Unbelief and sinfulness has led to many being "broken off" throughout the years. But even though there have been these periods of judgment, God has never forsaken the "trunk," his people, in history.

Third, the basis of Israel's failure is at the center of Paul's understanding of righteousness. Paul's own religious merits were of no use to him (Phil. 3:4–9). Judaism has the same problem. Merit with God cannot be found in something we can offer, something we conjure up out of our history or religion. God's righteousness works from our emptiness and thus is known to us as grace. If this is true, then Jews and Gentiles are equals (11:32), and Judaism cannot claim any historic privileges any more than Paul could. One cannot demand the promises of God—much less the land—based on religious privilege.[36] Paul writes about Israel:

> "I can testify that they have a zeal for God, but it is not enlightened. For, being ignorant of the righteousness that comes from God, and seeking to establish their own, they have not submitted to God's righteousness. For Christ is the end of the law so that there may be righteousness for everyone who believes." (Rom. 10:2–4)

Finally, Paul retains a special place for unbelieving Israel even though they are "broken off" from God's people. During the present time, Israel has become "hardened" (11:25), but in the future, after the Gentiles have been "grafted in," all Israel will be saved once more (11:26–27). Paul thus anticipates a future redemption in the plan of God that will include the Jewish people who originally rejected Christ. Israel might be reattached in the present era, but this can happen only through belief in Jesus (11:23). For the most part, Paul's hope for Israel is future, at the end of time.[37]

But more must be said. If Judaism remains—even in its brokenness—a people with a unique future, a people still to be redeemed, then it follows that they currently have a place of honor even in their unbelief. Note Paul's words in Romans 11:28–29: "As regards the gospel they are enemies of God for your sake; but as regards election they are beloved, for the sake of their ancestors; for the gifts and the calling of God are irrevocable."

Paul freely admits that Judaism now stands opposed to the gospel. Judaism is hostile to God's new purposes in Christ. Judaism has rejected the new covenant. Nevertheless, even in this disobedience, these broken branches still possess an incomparable place in history. Unbelieving Judaism is beloved, just as exiled Judaism was beloved in the Old Testament. Judaism holds an enduring role. For the sake of their history, for the sake of the promises made to their ancestors, God will retain a place for Jews in history. In their present condition of unbelief, they deserve honor. And when they accept Christ, be it now or in the future, their brokenness will be restored. Paul enjoys drawing out the metaphor of the olive tree to its limit. God is eager to see "these natural branches" grafted back in place. "For if you have been cut from what is by nature a wild olive tree and grafted, contrary to nature, into a cultivated olive tree, how much more will these natural branches be grafted back into their own olive tree" (Rom. 11:24).

Let us sum up. Few passages of Paul's writings have been more difficult than Romans 9–11. Interpreters are sharply divided in their understanding of Paul's double message: On the one hand, Israel has fallen and the church has assumed its privileges. On the other hand, Paul still holds out an ongoing place for Israel both in the present and in the future. Some Christians think that unbelieving Israel still lives today as heirs to Abraham's promises, that Christ's new covenant did not bring about an epoch-changing shift among God's people. This view seems to neglect much of Paul's teaching in Galatians and Romans about Christians as Abraham's heirs.

Still other Christians reject Israel altogether, making no allowances for the promises God made throughout the Scriptures. But Paul would find this view equally unsatisfying. As he says in Romans 11:29, "the gifts and the calling of God are irrevocable."

I prefer a middle position that harmonizes Paul's double commitment. Israel has fallen and has been utterly disobedient. Christians have been grafted into their place. Christians enjoy that place once held by Abraham. Indeed, Christians are the heirs of Abraham. And yet fallen Israel in its unbelief remains unique, honored, and beloved because of God's commitment to Israel's ancestors. Things have not changed. As God says through Isaiah, "I held out my hands all day long to a rebellious people" (Isa. 65:2). Yet Israel's obstinacy did not end God's affection for his people. The same is true today.[38]

CONCLUSION

Father George of Ramallah would tell us that the question "Who owns the land?" is not so simple. It is not just a matter of pointing to the promises of Abraham, identifying modern Israel as heirs to those promises, and then theologically justifying the Israeli claim to land. On the contrary, Christian theology demands that the true recipients of these promises might well include the Christian church. It may mean that the church alone receives these promises! Christian theology must at least take into account the new covenant of Christ and its implications for Israel.

It is clear from Romans 11 that unbelieving Israel still holds a place of honor. These "enemies of the gospel" are beloved. But this does not mean that Israel still holds a solitary place in relation to Abraham's promises. According to Christian teaching, Israel cannot make an exclusive claim to the land as if the new covenant had never happened. In fact, the New Testament refers to previous covenants as "obsolete" and "vanishing away" (Heb. 8:13).[39] Nor can Christians simply move from Abraham's promises in Genesis directly to modern Israel, skipping entirely what the New Testament says concerning Abraham's heritage. According to the New Testament, Christians are children of Abraham because this heritage is acquired by faith, not by lineage. In Christ, the promises of God are theirs.[40]

Imagine the implications that come with this result! Jewish settlers cannot eject Christian residents from Jerusalem saying, "The land is ours according to the Bible." If the Scriptures are to speak in full, the Christian Scriptures should be part of the conversation as well.

We also saw that the New Testament goes a long way toward spiritualizing the nature of these promises. That is, the Israelite endeavor to acquire land and forge a nation takes on a different shape in the new covenant of Christ. God's people no longer are called to build an empire based on the books of Genesis or Joshua. The Israeli attempt to take land and forge a nation is religiously misdirected. God's people are called to infiltrate the empires of the world, bringing the gospel of Jesus Christ to all, regardless of history, race, or religious persuasion.

NOTES

1. Beirut: Institute for Palestine Studies, 1970.

2. Personal interview, March 23, 1992.

3. See P. Richardson, *Israel in the Apostolic Church* (Cambridge: Cambridge Univ. Press, 1969), 1–32.

4. See W. D. Davies, *The Gospel and the Land. Early Christianity and Jewish Territorial Doctrine* (Berkeley: Univ. of California Press, 1974), and *The Territorial Dimension of Judaism* (Berkeley: Univ. of California Press, 1982; reprinted with a symposium and further reflections, Minneapolis: Fortress, 1991).

5. *Territorial Dimension of Judaism,* reprint ed., 19.

6. Ibid., 20, italics mine.

7. Ibid., 25.

8. Today the "Ninth of Ab" is still celebrated in Israel. On that evening Israel recalls the destruction of Jerusalem both by the Babylonians (586 B.C.) and by the Romans (A.D. 70). Jews customarily read the book of Lamentations aloud that night as a feature of their devotions.

9. This is especially clear as a motif in Matthew and Mark. See Davies, *Gospel and the Land,* 221–43.

10. This subject of the relationship between the New Testament and Israel is one of the most complex we have in biblical scholarship. The literature is vast. These pages will offer the barest summary.

11. This has been outlined brilliantly by a little-known book written by N. W. Lund, *Israel och Församlingen* (translated from Swedish by J. Eldon Johnson in his unpublished diss., "The Pauline Concept of Israel and the Church" [North Park Theological Seminary, 1960]).

12. A similar theme of a fruitless vineyard is found in Luke 13:6–9, where the same suggestion is given: the absence of fruit brings swift judgment.

13. W. Brueggemann, *The Land. Place as Gift, Promise, and Challenge in Biblical Faith* (Philadelphia: Fortress, 1977), 172–73.

14. Ibid., 171.

15. G. Ladd, *The Presence of the Future* (Grand Rapids: Eerdmans, 1974), 249.

16. Ibid., 250.

17. Students of Matthew commonly locate in this gospel hints that Jesus is a new Moses inaugurating a new Torah or law that fulfills and surpasses that found in the Old Testament.

18. For a full explanation of the remnant and Jesus' kingdom, see Ladd, *Presence of the Future*, 250–52. Note how in John 8, for instance, Jesus questions whether or not someone is *truly* a child of Abraham if he seeks to kill him (8:39–47). In some fashion, therefore, heritage from Abraham may be jeopardized. Divine status is not a question of bloodline but of faith.

19. Technically speaking, Jesus is not *gnostic* in the gospel of John.

20. *Gospel and the Land*, 316–18.

21. Ibid., 368.

22. John was written in Greek, and the Hebrew Old Testament was translated into Greek (called the Septuagint). The Greek word *skene* is the word used both in the Septuagint and in John for "tabernacle."

23. *Gospel and the Land*, 367.

24. W. Brueggemann, *The Land. Place as Gift, Promise, and Challenge in Biblical Faith*, 179.

25. H. Ridderbos outlines Paul's use of names for the church, thereby making the case that Paul believes that "the church is the continuation and fulfillment of the historical people of God that in Abraham God chose to himself from all peoples and to which he

bound himself by making the covenant and the promises." *Paul. An Outline of His Theology* (Grand Rapids: Eerdmans, 1975), 327.

26. Ibid., 178.

27. D. Guthrie, *Galatians,* New Century Bible (London: Oliphants, 1974), 102. Similarly, see J. Schniewind and G. Friedrich, "Christ is the true heir of the promise, of the universal inheritance, and determines the fellow-heirs," *Theological Dictionary of the New Testament,* 10 vols. (Grand Rapids: Eerdmans, 1964–76), 2:583, cited in R.Y.K. Fung, *The Epistle to the Galatians* (Grand Rapids: Eerdmans, 1988), 156.

28. Considerable debate surrounds the interpretation of this verse. See any commentary and especially P. Richardson, *Israel in the Apostolic Church* (Cambridge: Cambridge Univ. Press, 1969), 74–84.

29. Ibid., 173.

30. Ibid., 174.

31. This is likewise done in Revelation 21:9–14, where the church bears the names of both the apostles and the tribes of Israel.

32. Paul illustrates this notion of the remnant using Elijah's story from 1 Kings 19. See Romans 9:6–11 and 9:27.

33. H. L. Ellison, *The Mystery of Israel. An Exposition of Romans 9–11.* (Grand Rapids: Eerdmans, 1966), 73–76; cf. J. Piper, *The Justification of God. An Exegetical and Theological Study of Romans 9:1–23* (Grand Rapids: Baker, 1983).

34. Paul inserts the Greek word "there" (*ekei*) to the Hosea citation to underscore the place of this new identity for gentiles. The place will be within Israel itself. See J. Munck, *Christ and Israel. An Interpretation of Romans 9–11* (Philadelphia: Fortress, 1967), 12, 72–73.

35. The sharpest place where Paul describes judgment on Israel is found in 1 Thessalonians 2:14–16: "For you, brothers and sisters, became imitators of the churches of God in Christ Jesus that are in Judea, for you suffered the same things from your own compatriots as they did from the Jews, who killed both the Lord Jesus and the prophets, and drove us out; they displease God and oppose everyone by hindering us from speaking to the Gentiles so that they may be saved. Thus they have constantly been filling up the measure of their sins; but God's wrath has overtaken them at last."

36. E. Käsemann, "Paul and Israel," in *New Testament Questions of Today* (Philadelphia: Fortress, 1969), 184. "For since Easter it has become clear that God's dealings are with all people and that Israel's election in days of yore points forward beyond Israel into that comprehensive history which began with Adam. There is no privilege in the face of God's omnipotence" (185).

37. G. E. Ladd, *A Theology of the New Testament* (Grand Rapids: Eerdmans, 1974), 561–63.

38. This fact of Israel's beloved place should challenge even the slightest hint of anti-Semitism in the church.

39. Hebrews makes this theme abundantly clear. See Hebrews 7:18, 19: "There is, on the one hand, the abrogation of an earlier commandment because it was weak and ineffectual (for the law made nothing perfect); there is, on the other hand, the introduction of a better hope, through which we approach God." Similarly Hebrews 9:15 explains the new covenant with reference to "a former covenant." The surpassing glory of the new covenant completely replaces that of the old covenant. Hebrews likely has in mind thoughts originally penned in Jeremiah 31 on God's coming covenant.

40. Some Christians have argued, on the other hand, that Israel and the church coexist, each enjoying different blessings. Israel obtains the material promises of Abraham and the old covenant, the church obtains the promises of Christ. The two will not merge into one body until the end of the age.

Chapter Eight

THE PALESTINIAN CHURCH

"The reason Jesus' words had struck me was this: Suddenly I knew that the first step toward reconciling Jew and Palestinian was the restoration of human dignity. Justice and righteousness were what I had been thirsting for." (E. Chacour, *Blood Brothers*, 146)[1]

"I give Christianity ten to fifteen years in Jordan and the West Bank and no more." (Bishop Elia Khoury, exiled Christian pastor, Amman, Jordan, 1990)

The cover of David Dolan's recent popular book on the Middle East is a telling portrayal of how we have come to view the problem of Israel/Palestine.[2] Its artwork shows two fists fiercely crashing across a map of the region. One fist has a star of David emblazoned on its wrist. The other shows the crescent of Islam tattooed prominently in red. What the artist omitted unveils a deeper neglect and misunderstanding not only in Dolan's book, but throughout our churches. No cross appears among the religious symbols of the Middle East. The conflict in Israel/Palestine is not between Judaism and Islam. It is among brothers, tribes we might say, whose struggle is comprehensive and includes culture, nationalism, and religion.

Not all Palestinians are Muslims. Of a worldwide Palestinian population of 4 to 5 million, about 10 percent, or about 450,000 people, are Christians.[3] But what about inside Israel/-

Palestine? Salim Munayer, dean of Bethlehem Bible College, notes that within the borders of pre-1967 Israel, about 107,000 Palestinian Arabs are Christians and these are found chiefly in Galilee.[4] In the West Bank there are approximately 7000 to 9000 Christians and another 7000 in Jerusalem. Thus in Israel/Palestine altogether, most observers believe there are about 120,000 Palestinian Christians. Remarkably—because Palestinian Christians have had greater freedom to emigrate—they are leaving in large numbers and now there may be as many as 400,000 Arab Christians living outside the country. The United States typically has a large Palestinian Christian community.

In Israel/Palestine, Greek Catholic (Melkite) Christians are the largest group, with about 45,000 members, followed by Greek Orthodox with 35,000. There are also Roman Catholics, Anglicans or Episcopalians (known as "the Protestants"), Baptists, Armenian Orthodox, and many other groups. There are also many evangelicals, such as the well-known Baptist church in Nazareth. The Anglican priest in Nablus is charismatic. Nazareth is even home to an evangelical Bible school for correspondence study which distributes more than eight hundred Arabic New Testaments every year.[5]

These facts surprise many American tourists as well as Israelis. Once when I was explaining this to a group of Jewish settlers on the West Bank, they blinked and accused me of being in error! "Palestinians are Muslims—or else they are not Palestinians! Maybe these Arabs are from the West!" they said. Nothing could be further from the truth. There has been a continuous Arab Christian population in Palestine for almost two thousand years. In fact, the book of Acts tells us that Arabs were present on the Day of Pentecost (Acts 2:11)!

Most Palestinian Christians reside in the cities of Bethlehem, Jerusalem, Ramallah, and Nazareth, where there are sizable Christian populations and strong churches. Others are in predominantly Muslim cities like Nablus. Father Yousef Sa'adeh pastors his Greek-Catholic (Melkite) congregation in Nablus, where each Sunday 50 people gather for worship. Nablus has about 120,000 residents but no more than 750 are Christians!

Christian villages can also be found. The city of Jenin (near

Nablus) consists of about eighty villages. Zababdi is one of a handful of villages in the mix that has three Christian communities: Protestant, Roman Catholic, and Greek Orthodox. Of Zababdi's 3000 residents, almost half are Christians. Beit Sahour, a town outside of Bethlehem, is host to the famed biblical "Shepherd's Fields." It has more than 10,000 people, most of whom are Christians.

These people have a voice that is yet to be heard by the West. Narratives of struggle and suffering have appeared (such as Elias Chacour's *Blood Brothers* and Audeh Rantisi's *Blessed Are the Peacemakers*). And the first Palestinian Christian theology has been written in English (Naim Ateek, *Justice and Only Justice*). In 1992 a choir of nineteen Palestinian Christian voices was published as *Faith and the Intifada*.[6] It is a record of the dilemma these Christians are facing on all levels of life—from religious freedom to economic survival.

The pastors of Palestinian churches minister to people who face the daily oppression of military occupation and who live with feelings of anger, resentment, powerlessness, and despair. Nadia Abboushi is a mother and a musician in Ramallah where she attends the Anglican church. "I never realized life could be so difficult," she says. "There is constant stress; constant agony. Raising children takes thought, maturity, and political awareness. I tell them that this situation is abnormal— life is not like this. But they ask, 'What is normal?' "[7] On Easter day, 1991, her sixteen-year-old son was shot at and arrested by the Israeli army while he was walking to his relatives' home in town. After paying a $250 fine, he was freed, but the wound of the unjust episode still haunts the family.

THREE CONCERNS OF PALESTINIAN CHRISTIANS

Palestinian Christians face formidable challenges as they work to understand their own identity in the Middle East. One pastor in Bethlehem asked me, "How do you lead a youth group when two of its leading members are being tortured in Israeli prison camps?" Christian high school students must learn to make suffering a part of their discipleship—a type of discipleship described throughout the New Testament.

Even using the Bible in their church has become a hurdle. Naim Ateek, a Jerusalem pastor, remarks, "Western Christians and many religious Jews were using the same Bible as we, but claiming to take from it a revelation from God that justified the conquest of our land and the extermination of our people."[8] Ateek is right. If the Bible is used as a vehicle of death and destruction by those who rule—if it is the Bible that kills you— it is hard to make it a source of light and life in congregational life.

Ateek's point was made clear to me in 1992 when I spent a night at Settlement Beth El north of Jerusalem and in the evening joined a discussion group with Jewish settlers who were chiefly from New York. For them, Israel's treatment of the Arabs was biblically justified as a form of conquest. They defended intelligently the notion of a state with unequal citizens. One man remarked, "Arabs are different than us, do not possess inalienable rights, and should always be second-class citizens." The key here is that today this claim is being made for theological reasons. Israeli "apartheid" is being anchored in the Bible. This is deeply troubling to everyone who uses the Scriptures in the Middle East. It is deeply troubling for Christian churches.

Three concerns can be heard from Bethlehem to Nazareth among the Palestinian Christians. As an American believer I cannot help but pause and listen. These people are my brothers and sisters in Christ. They are the ones whose ancestors nurtured Christian faith as it was first preached centuries ago. It is to them that I am indebted for my own faith.

A Plea for Visibility and Fellowship

Munir Fasheh, a professor of education at Bir Zeit University in Ramallah, has made the case that Palestinian Christians are invisible to us.[9] Fasheh is right. When tourists and pilgrims visit the Holy Land, they frequently show surprise when meeting Arab Christians. "When did you become a Christian?" is a question that Palestinian Christians hear regularly. And it wounds them deeply. The question presupposes that Arabs are anything but Christians—Muslims most likely—and that some Western evangelist brought them salvation.[10]

Worse still is the treatment given to Arab Christians by evangelicals who ought to know better. In May 1990 I interviewed Mr. Johann Luckhoff, the director of the International Christian Embassy in Jerusalem. When I asked him about the Palestinian Christians, his answer was to the point: "They're not really Christians anyway. Christianity for Arabs is just a political commitment."[11] Obviously he had never prayed or worshiped with any of the thousands of Christians in this land.

To be sure, as an American evangelical I have to avoid weighing a Middle Easterner's faith in my cultural terms. His or her spiritual culture is different than mine. James Stamoolis, dean of the graduate school at Wheaton College, has written about this in detail.[12] The Eastern churches did not inherit the contributions of Augustine or Aquinas or Luther that have shaped our Western faith. Theirs is a different history equal to ours in every way. When an Arab Greek Orthodox grandmother from Nazareth says that Christ is her only hope each day, I will not be cynical about her faith. I am not called to be her judge simply because she prefers incense to the hymns of Isaac Watts.

In March 1992 I interviewed Jim Schultz, an attorney working at the International Christian Embassy. When asked about Arab Christians, his first response was telling: "But are they really born-again Christians?" His implication was clearly that they were not. I further asked how I could tell if someone was "filled with the Spirit" in this culture. He replied, "The first fruit of the Spirit here is a love for Israel and the Jewish people." Never before have I heard such an unwillingness to listen for the integrity of someone else's faith in different cultural terms.

Palestinian Christians want us to embrace them as equals and invite them into fellowship. They want their Christian life to be acknowledged and respected. But it is not as if our acknowledgment in some way makes their faith authentic. Their Christian tradition has a life and validity apart from Western recognition. Arab Christians have been living in the Middle East for two thousand years and have survived more oppression and grief than we can imagine. No. They wish to be received with the honor befitting the churches that gave the West its Christianity.

A Cry for Justice

Christ Evangelical Episcopal Church in Nazareth is the largest Protestant congregation in the country. Behind the altar at the front is a beautiful Arabic inscription that has served as the motto of the church since its founding in 1871. Nazareth is the city where Jesus not only grew up, but where he announced his ministry and messiahship. This announcement is found in Luke 4:18–19:

> "The Spirit of the Lord is upon me,
>   because he has anointed me
>   to bring good news to the poor.
> He has sent me to proclaim release to the captives
>   and recovery of sight to the blind,
>   to let the oppressed go free,
> to proclaim the year of the Lord's favor."

Today this text has a profound meaning. As Deacon (Reverend) Zahi Nassir explained to me, the words tell us something about Jesus' sense of mission. Jesus had the poor, the captive, the blind, and the oppressed on his mind. I worshiped one Sunday at this Palestinian church and thought about these words as the congregation sang Charles Wesley's hymn "Love Divine, All Loves Excelling" in a splendid Arabic translation. The hymn echoes the vision of the verse: that God's salvation would be complete, not just securing our eternal destiny but also giving us a life graced with deliverance from *all* evil and suffering.

Most Palestinian pastors take these verses from Luke 4 seriously. For them the problem of living in a country where discrimination runs rampant, where government policy is overtly unfair, and where the systems of justice are often not available has shaped their ministry. When a family's land is confiscated, when a parish home is blown up without a good reason, or when a member of the youth group disappears into the Israeli military prison system, life cannot go on as before.

Palestinian Christians are looking to us for support. They

claim that they are reliving for the first time in history the conditions of the first-century church, in which a Christian minority is suffering under the rule of a Jewish majority. We in the West are the Christians of the diaspora, or dispersion. And our support is needed. In the very same way, on his third missionary tour, the apostle Paul gathered the support of the Greek Christians for the Middle Eastern church, which was sorely oppressed (see 1 Cor. 16:1–4; 2 Cor. 8:1–15; 2 Thess. 2:13–16).

If there is a Bible passage that has become pivotal to the Palestinian Christian experience, it is the story of Ahab and the vineyard of Naboth from 1 Kings 21 (discussed in chapter 4). It is pivotal because it addresses the most profound injustice of all: the theft of land. Israel's excuses of national security, expediency, and primary domain are all compared with Ahab's plot to steal Naboth's vineyard. This is the biblical touchstone that is dear to the Palestinian heart.

Another important story is that of Zacchaeus in Luke 19.[13] Zacchaeus had been a dishonest tax collector, cheating the people of their livelihoods. Jesus announced that salvation had come to Zacchaeus's house. Jesus had seen evidence of Zacchaeus's new moral life: the thief had been restoring all that he had stolen and giving added compensation besides. This story is extremely important for Palestinians. Proof of godly righteousness is seen in repentance and restoration of things stolen. Israel is stealing the land and the livelihoods of many of its people.

In Nazareth, the reality of land loss is at the forefront of everyone's thinking. Nazareth is at the bottom of a "bowl" in the mountains of Galilee. In 1948 it had 3,336 acres with a population of 15,000 people. Today the population has risen to 55,000, and the land has been reduced to 1,668 acres. Almost 50 percent of the town has been taken! The southeastern hills of Nazareth (called "Elite Nazareth") has all been confiscated for Israeli development. Prominent Arab Christian families still own their useless property deeds and forever live looking up at their lost land.

A Historic Claim to Residence

Riah Abu El-Assal, an Anglican pastor in Nazareth,[14] despairs when he hears arguments for land ownership based on Jewish claims coming from the Bible. He feels that American Christians are often given the following scenario, which is one of the great myths of the Middle East: The Jews owned the land throughout the Old Testament era, were exiled by the Romans in A.D. 70, and in their absence, Arabs moved into the region sometime in the seventh century under the inspiration of Mohammed. Now the Arab interlude is over. The Jews have come home—and therefore the Arab residents with no historic tenure cannot make historic claims to land and residence.

El-Assal, however, once taught Islamics and is today one of the leading Palestinian Christian intellectuals. He makes two points. First, "Arab" is a racial designation of people throughout the Middle East. Arab "Jews" were commonplace in antiquity.[15] Even in the Old Testament, the incorporation of such non-Jews into Israel was common. Jethro was a Midianite (neighbors to the Arabs), and his daughter became Moses' wife (Ex. 2:15, 22). We would be hard-pressed to distinguish Jethro from any other Middle Easterner today. In fact, Judaism reached India (as did Christianity) via Arabia, where Jewish Arabs lived and traveled. When Israel was exiled in A.D. 70, Jews fled to these Jewish Arab communities in Arabia, Iraq, Egypt, and the Persian Gulf.[16] Therefore Arabs were well-acquainted with Judaism, and many of them were Jewish believers throughout the Middle East.

This leads to El-Assal's second and most important point. Arab Jews were among those converted to Christ in the earliest church. Acts 2:11 specifically includes Arabs as among those Jews converted on Pentecost. "This is my lineage," he asserts. "I came from Arab Jews who accepted faith in Christ. I was not an observer at someone else's festival at Pentecost. It was my festival too."[17] Early historians tell us that Thomas carried the gospel to the Arab tribes. Then, as so often happened in the Middle East, entire tribes were converted to Christ once the tribal chieftain took on the faith. "Many became priests and bishops, and some are named among the saints of the church. . . . hundreds of them were martyred in the cause of the Christian faith."[18]

Most recently Kenneth Cragg, a scholar of Islamics and Middle Eastern history, has published a definitive book, *The Arab Christian: A History of the Middle East.* Cragg supplies ample evidence—from the visits of church dignitaries who met Arab Christians to ancient Arab Christian poetry—to show the existence of an indigenous church in the region.[19]

My point is this: If land promises come to Judaism by virtue of tenure in the land and biblical promise, Arab Jews (El-Assal's heritage) gain these promises as well, and their faith in Jesus does not invalidate their claim to Jewish ancestry. If we ask, Where did the Arab Christians come from? the answer clearly begins with the Day of Pentecost. Hence Arabs are not "late-comers" to the scene in Israel/Palestine even though over the centuries their culture has absorbed cultural features of Islam. Jewish-Christian communities grew, and Arab-Jews were in their ranks. They were among the very earliest Christian communities we know, and they have been living in the Middle East continually ever since.[20]

SUMMARY

As evangelicals look at the complex problems of Israel/Palestine, it is apparent that we have neglected an entire community. We have been eager to support Israel's life and future but in doing so have neglected Christ's ancient church in the cities of his birth, childhood, and ministry. For instance, tourists visit Nazareth for such a brief period that their buses remain lined up on the main street in front of the Church of the Annunciation. Tour guides keep the visit short: thirty minutes for the Catholic Church and thirty minutes for the bathroom and shopping. That's it! The Palestinian Christians are wounded by the "sixty-minute visit" in which the "living stones" of Christ's living church are overlooked.

Worse yet, Christians in Israel/Palestine are suffering. Particularly in the West Bank and Gaza (but also elsewhere) they are discriminated against, oppressed, and imprisoned in their own country. During the Intifada the leaders of Jerusalem's churches sought to make a joint pronouncement to declare January 24–31, 1988, a "week of prayer" for peace and justice. Israeli censors forbade the churches from publishing their statement in the Israeli or Arab media.[21]

In another incident, in May 1988, the Jerusalem Baptist Church called Rev. Alex Awad to be its pastor. He had no criminal or political record, he was a pacifist, and he had excellent American academic credentials and held a sterling record as a faculty member at Bethlehem Bible College. Yet the Israelis found "visa irregularities" in his case in order to stop his ministry. Rev. Riah Abu El-Assal, whose thoughts I outlined above, was forbidden to leave the country for years and has frequently been quarantined to his home city—all this because he has been a community leader who as a Christian has spoken up for justice among his people. He sought to protect the sheep of his flock.

The situation among the Palestinian Christians is becoming so critical that there is a virtual exodus of people leaving the country. Bishop Ignatius IV calls it "the emptying of Christianity from the Middle East."[22] In Ramallah and Bethlehem in 1948 each community was 90 percent Christian. Today each community is only 50 percent Christian. Christian leaders speak frequently of "the museumification" of the church. Soon the living church of Israel/Palestine may be gone with only museum-like buildings left for Christian tourists.

It is time American evangelicals stood in solidarity with the church of the Middle East. It is time for us to embrace and support Palestinian Christians in their desperate struggle for survival. They are our brothers and sisters in Christ.

NOTES

1. Old Tappan, N.J.: Revell, 1984.

2. *Holy War for the Promised Land. Israel's Struggle to Survive in the Muslim Middle East* (Nashville: Nelson, 1991).

3. Naim Ateek, *Justice and Only Justice* (Maryknoll, N.Y.: Orbis, 1989), 4.

4. Salim Munayer, "Arab Palestinian Christians in the Holy Land," unpublished paper printed in Jerusalem. Munayer is a

graduate of Fuller Seminary (Pasadena, Calif.), dean of the faculty at Bethlehem Bible College, and a specialist in ministry among Muslims. His statistics were taken from *The Statistical Abstract of Israel 1990* (no. 41), Central Bureau of Statistics, Israel.

5. Emmaus Bible School, George Khalil, Director, Box 240, Nazareth 16101, Israel.

6. *Faith and the Intifada. Palestinian Christian Voices*, ed. Naim S. Ateek, Marc H. Ellis, and Rosemary Radford Ruether (Maryknoll, N.Y.: Orbis, 1992).

7. Personal interview, March 24, 1992.

8. Ateek, *Justice*, 3.

9. *Faith and the Intifada*, 61–63.

10. See the remarkable stories of J. and M. Hefley, *Arabs, Christians and Jews. They Want Peace Now!* (Plainfield, N.J.: Logos, 1978), 25–37.

11. Personal interview, May 29, 1990. In an interview with *Cornerstone* magazine, Jan Willem van Der Hoeven at the embassy stereotyped all Palestinians as "evil, knife-wielding terrorists" (*Cornerstone* 21, no. 100 [1992]: 24).

12. J. J. Stamoolis, *Easter Orthodox Mission Theology Today*, American Society of Missiology Series, no. 10 (Maryknoll, N.Y.: Orbis, 1986).

13. This was explained to me by Dr. Mitri Raheb, professor of Church History, Bethlehem Bible College, March 31, 1992.

14. Riah Abu El-Assal is actually archdeacon of the Jerusalem Diocese of the Episcopal Church, Nazareth.

15. It is also important to remember that Jews and Arabs are racially *both* Semites or descendants of Shem, Noah's son. It is a misnomer, therefore, to say that an Arab is "anti-Semitic."

16. When Mohammed came to the scene six hundred years later, Medina's largest tribe was Jewish! Mohammed originally told his followers to pray in the direction of Jerusalem! But because the early church in Arabia would not incorporate his reforms and accept his leadership, Islam was born. Hence, according to El-Assal, early Christianity bears some responsibility for the rise of the Islamic faith.

17. Personal interview, March 28, 1992.

18. Riah Abu El-Assal, "The Identity of the Palestinian Christian in Israel," in *Faith and the Intifada*, 78–79. El-Assal is currently working on a manuscript that will explain his thesis in detail. It will quickly become a landmark study for the Palestinian Christian identity.

19. K. Cragg, *The Arab Christian. A History of the Middle East* (Louisville: Westminster/John Knox, 1991), 31–51; cf. J. Trimingham,

Christianity Among the Arabs in Pre-Islamic Times (New York: Longman, 1979). Irfan Shahid has completed a series of academic studies outlining Arab life in the pre-Islamic centuries. See his Rome and the Arabs in the Third Century (Washington: Dumbarton Oaks, 1980), Byzantium and the Arabs in the Fourth Century (Washington: Dumbarton Oaks, 1984), and Byzantium and the Arabs in the Fifth Century (Washington: Dumbarton Oaks, 1990).

20. This view outlined in these paragraphs is hotly disputed particularly among the Christian Zionists in Israel. See C. Wagner. "The Palestinization of Jesus," Dispatch from Jerusalem 17.1 (1992), 1.

21. D. Wagner, "Holy Land Christians and Survival," in Faith and the Intifada, 48. Wagner's copy of the prayer was sent out of the country illegally to him by FAX.

22. Ibid., 43.

Chapter Nine

LIVING STONES
IN THE LAND

"Four years after our flight from Lydda I dedicated my life
to the service of Jesus Christ. Like me and my fellow
refugees, Jesus had lived in adverse circumstances, often
with only a stone for a pillow. They tortured and killed him
in Jerusalem, only ten miles from Ramallah, my new home.
He was the victim of terrible indignities. Nevertheless, Jesus
prayed on behalf of those who engineered his death,
'Father, forgive them. . . .' Can I do less?" (Audeh Rantisi,
Blessed Are the Peacemakers, 26)[1]

I struggle, wondering how best to describe the vitality and
wonder of the Palestinian Christians. I could do it statistically,
reporting that there are about 8 million Arabic-speaking Christians, and then recite statistics outlining the number of people
in each Palestinian denomination. But I would prefer to take
you with me to an Arabic worship service in East Jerusalem.

St. George's Arabic service begins at 9:30 A.M. The last
Sunday I attended I was given an English photocopy of the
great hymn, "My Jesus, I Love Thee," and I sang the English
words as the congregation used an Arabic text:

> My Jesus I love Thee, I know Thou art mine,
> For Thee all the follies of sin I resign;
> My gracious Redeemer, my Saviour art Thou;
> If ever I loved Thee, my Jesus, 'tis now.

The sermon was about the struggle of keeping families together in a world of shifting moral values. After the service, Arabic coffee was served as usual in the parlor, and eager hands reached out to greet visitors in the name of Christ.

To sing hymns with an Arabic tempo, to kneel in communion with Palestinians, to have the words "This is my body, broken for you" spoken in Arabic by the priest, and then to learn over coffee about profound struggle—these are experiences I would offer to any who would know the Palestinian Christians. As pilgrims and tourists, we often enter this land to see archaeological stones. The churches of the Holy Land would have us come see them too, the "living stones" of the land, as they like to be described.

As American evangelicals, the most compelling reason to stand in unity with the Palestinian church comes from meeting Palestinian Christians themselves. Some are preserving ancient Eastern rites which I barely understand. Some have deep and vibrant testimonies that put to shame the weak-kneed Christianity that so often inhabits Western churches. These are Christians whose faith has been tested and honed through centuries of struggle. For more than four hundred years the Ottoman Empire would not even let them ring their church bells. To be sure, these churches are not perfect. Critics will at once point to examples of worldliness and compromise. But no church in the world is perfect, much less ours.

The following is a sample list of Palestinian Christians—living stones—in Israel/Palestine. Countless more names could be added. Some are heroic in faith, others are quiet believers. Some have suffered so profoundly that their faith has been shaken to its core, and they would hesitate to be listed in these pages. Here I offer them as an introduction, an invitation, to meet more of the thousands of Arab Christians just like them.

SELWA DIABIS, RAMALLAH, BUSINESS ENTREPRENEUR

Selwa was born in Nazareth in 1960, and because her father was a minister, their family moved more often than the average Arab family, first to Haifa and then to Nablus. As a teenager she grew up in a conservative Muslim community in which she had a limited number of friends and learned that as a Christian she was different. She graduated from Bir Zeit University (north of Ramallah) in 1978 with a biochemistry major. After graduation she became involved in illiteracy programs and began teaching public health to village teachers. Today she lives in Ramallah, a short drive north of Jerusalem.

Young, fashionable, and bright, Selwa entered a unique enterprise called Mattin in 1983. Mattin is a Palestinian nonprofit development company that makes women's pure silk lingerie for the internationally marketed Layal line. Their products have been sold in Harrods (London), Fenwicks, Victoria's Secret, Bloomingdale's, and Bonwit Teller as well as advertised in *Vogue*, *Marie Claire*, and *Elle*. Export volume reached $30,000 per month in 1990 as Mattin employed forty Palestinian women in professional garment construction.

But today Mattin is in court, and all exports have stopped. Because they used labels that said, "Made in the Israeli-Occupied West Bank" the government put a halt to their work by denying them an export/import license.[2] But Selwa is not discouraged. Mattin is "experimental." It is designed to teach Palestinian women skills and to test the Israeli controls on Arab business. She calls it "a form of economic resistance." A phalanx of young attorneys works around the corner at Al Haq, a Palestinian legal/human rights group. They are Selwa's good friends and allies.

Selwa's work springs from the Christian foundation laid down year after year in her family.[3] But the true test of Christian faith does not consist in words or church attendance, Selwa says, even though she is a very active Episcopalian. For Selwa Diabis, Christian faith and practical works of service are inseparably linked. Her life—as her work—is being lived sacrificially, as she helps the Palestinian women of Ramallah. I asked her what fuels her efforts, and she replied, "The well-being and happiness of the people around me feed me."[4] And more than once, her safety—even her life itself—has been at risk by those in power who feel threatened by her efforts.

MITRI RAHEB, BETHLEHEM, PASTOR, PROFESSOR

As a young Christian intellectual, Mitri's Ph.D. from Marburg University (Germany) and the caliber of his professorial work stand up to international standards of scholarship.[5] He not only teaches church history at Bethlehem Bible College, but he also is pastor of the Evangelical Lutheran Christmas Church in Bethlehem (founded in 1854). There each Sunday about fifty-five families gather for worship and forty children study in Sunday school. Four youth groups and about fifty women in "fellowship circles" make the church one of the liveliest in Bethlehem.

Mitri likes to explain that his Christian family can chronicle its presence in Bethlehem as far back as a thousand years. "Raheb" means "monk" in Arabic, and one valley near Bethlehem bearing this name was owned by his ancestors. But the history goes back even further than this. Five Jewish-Christian families (whom Mitri can name) lived in Bethlehem just after the New Testament was written, and they are the great, great ancestors of Christianity in this city. Remarkably these families are still in Bethlehem to this day. Other Christians came later—especially with the Crusades, but the Raheb family reaches back to the earliest believing communities of Christendom. As heir to the faith of these earliest "Jewish-Christian" believers in the Holy Land, Mitri is amazed by those who would deny his identity and history.

A few moments with Mitri, however, and it is clear that he is living with his people in the midst of their suffering. I interviewed Mitri in 1992, and as I inquired about the sorts of things he has experienced as a pastor, he told me about two elders, ages thirty-five and forty-five, who each spent twenty-one months in prison without being formally charged. Their families—without incomes—have suffered terribly. Another elder has had large portions of his land confiscated by the Israelis because, they said, "the land is uncultivated." Actually they took the land for an illegal new West Bank settlement. The army will not reimburse him.

Perhaps the most powerful moment of my interview with Mitri came when he unfolded an old letter from his wallet. It was so brittle that it crackled. It was written by a young man who was a leader in Mitri's youth group while the young man was imprisoned in Ansar III, an army prison famous for brutal torture. The smuggled note is clearly sacred script for Mitri. He explains that it is a "letter of faith written under imprisonment—much like the letters of the New Testament." In the letter the boy describes the awesome physical torture he has endured. He calls his prison "the slaughterhouse." Then he goes on to interpret Isaiah 53 as an explanation of his suffering. But this is not the remarkable thing. The bulk of the letter consists of five suggestions on how Mitri might improve the youth group. In the midst of his profound suffering, the young man has the needs of the church on his mind. I couldn't help but think of Paul in Philippians 2.

Mitri wonders if any pastor can be equipped for this sort of calling. But clearly God has given this young man gifts not listed in any seminary catalog. "Living in this situation makes you mature," he says. "Either you emigrate from this place—or you stay and witness the righteousness of God at work."[6]

JONATHAN KHUTTAB, JERUSALEM, ATTORNEY

The challenge that confronts most Christian professionals in Israel/Palestine is how they might employ their expertise in order to assist the struggle of the Palestinian people in practical ways. Physicians might serve those who cannot pay or might volunteer in impoverished areas. Educators and social workers sometimes work with refugee camps. As an internationally respected attorney, Jonathan Khuttab has confronted the Israeli occupation in the courts and in the press.

Jonathan received his B.A. degree at the evangelical Messiah College in Pennsylvania in 1973 and obtained a doctorate in law from the University of Virginia in 1977. For two years (until 1979) he practiced law in New York, becoming a member of the New York bar. In 1980 he returned to Israel/Palestine, joined the Israeli bar, and began studying Hebrew. Today he is one of the most respected attorneys in Jerusalem. His understanding of the political crisis of his country is so keen that he frequently appears in interviews on

CBS, ABC, NBC, and CNN. He has appeared more than once with Ted Koppel on ABC's "Nightline."

In addition to his law practice and his active involvement at St. George's Episcopalian Church in East Jerusalem, Jonathan founded two organizations that today stand for justice in Palestine. The first, Al Haq (in Arabic, *The Truth*) is a human rights research and publications organization. Al Haq's forty employees compile courtroom-quality documentation of human rights abuses throughout Israel, the West Bank, and Gaza.[7] Its support comes through major grants from Western churches, the Ford Foundation, and many other sources. Its list of publications offers an impressive record of Israel's treatment of the Palestinians since 1948.

Jonathan's second and newest endeavor is called The Mandella Institute. Here he is working for the care of needy Palestinian political prisoners, their civil rights, their medical needs, any basic provisions for their comfort (such as warm clothes and blankets in winter). Mandella even supplies paper and books for them. But above all, it works for visitation rights so that families may see their imprisoned sons and fathers regularly. Visitation is always a problem, and generally attorneys and pastors are denied access to those in their care. Jonathan is working to change this.

In 1992 I asked Jonathan why he started these programs. His answer: "Christians should have the Lordship of Christ throughout their lives."[8] For him, this includes social needs and political justice as well. "Attitudes toward our enemies, toward suffering, toward the world—these should all be addressed by our Christianity."[9]

Jonathan exemplifies the ultimate expression of the committed Christian layperson. He is a high-profile change agent in his community who has brought professional expertise and Christian compassion together. The week I visited him, he was running to and from the Augusta Victoria Hospital in Jerusalem. A team of American surgeons from Norfolk, Virginia's, "Operation Smile" was doing free cleft lip/palate surgeries for poor Arab families. Typically, Jonathan was the head of the local committee sponsoring them. He could frequently be heard standing in the hospital halls, translating Arabic and English for frightened Palestinian families as surgeons explained the progress of the children.

JAD ISAAC, BEIT-SAHOUR, AGRICULTURAL BIOLOGIST

When the Intifada began, the Christian village of Beit-Sahour outside Bethlehem suddenly found itself in the spotlight. Palestinians everywhere decided to "disengage" from the Israeli economy, and this meant refusing to purchase even Israeli agricultural products. In 1988 Jad Isaac was an associate professor of Plant Physiology at Bethlehem University. He and a group of his friends all loved gardening and used their professional expertise to teach their neighbors how to build small family "plots" (of 200 square meters) that would intensively raise enough food (vegetables, fruit, and livestock) to support one family. Virtually overnight almost ten thousand Arabs were buying gardening products from "The Shed"—an outlet for seeds brought up from Jericho. Charitable contributions subsidized the seeds, giving even the poor an opportunity to build gardens. In March 1988 alone, 200,000 seedlings—tomato, eggplant, pepper, cauliflower, and lettuce—were distributed along with 1000 fruit trees, 4000 chickens, 8 lambs, pesticides, drip irrigation equipment, and farming gear. The *Jerusalem Post* called the work "a quiet kind of uprising." Journalists flocked to the village—as did Palestinians from all over the West Bank. Soon "Intifada gardens" were spreading from home to home like wildfire.

That is, until June 1988. Citing "state security" the Israeli army closed everything down in Beit Sahour. But Jad knew that it was coming. This was an incredibly successful form of resistance, and the international press loved it. His picture appeared in newspapers from the *Washington Post* to the *Manchester Guardian*. From May 17 until June 5, Jad was arrested daily by the army—generally at night. Harassment continued for the leadership committee until finally "The Shed" had to close. Then on July 8, 1988, Jad was arrested and taken for five months to the dreaded Ansar III prison camp.[10]

Jad speaks haltingly about the experience. Its scars still haunt him. Being a strong leader, he quickly found himself in charge of the prison pharmacy. He studied Hebrew and taught fellow prisoners ecology, economics, politics, and English.[11] He even taught the structure of DNA by using bread-bag wires as models. Academic papers were penned on the inside of wrappers from cigarette boxes.

"For the first time," Jad said, "I understood suffering." He experienced torture and food deprivation and extreme fatigue. He lost weight dramatically. And on August 17 of that year he watched three Palestinians be shot dead for refusing to build a prison fence. When he describes the event, his voice still shakes with anger.

In fact, righteous anger floods Jad's soul. He feels profound disillusionment with his Greek Orthodox tradition, which, he feels, has not taken a sufficiently active role in promoting the needs of the poor. Human values and human dignity are at the core of his Christian upbringing, and the church has failed to defend it.

Today Jad is no longer at Bethlehem University. He is doing research at Applied Research Development, an agricultural research group in Bethlehem. He is still active in promoting peace and justice. He helped found The Rapprochement Centre in Beit Sahour, where young Palestinians and Israelis can meet on neutral turf and talk about their differences. But Jad does not attend church. For him the Christian church has no credibility until it courageously confronts the pain and injustices of his homeland.

SALIM MUNAYER, BETHLEHEM,
PROFESSOR, COLLEGE ADMINISTRATOR

On the righthand side of the main road through Bethlehem, the road that connects Jerusalem with Hebron, travelers can see the campus of Bethlehem Bible College, an undiscovered jewel on the West Bank. Founded in 1979, "BBC" and its president, Bishara Awad, are providing an interdenominational, evangelical college curriculum for Palestine's future church leaders. One visit convinces even the casual visitor that here is a ministry whose importance can only grow over the years.

Salim Munayer serves as the college's dean. His vision for the college has been shaped by his study at Fuller Seminary's School of World Missions. There Salim worked to understand how the gospel can be conveyed more effectively to the followers of Islam. As a result of his research, he co-authored *The New Creation Book for Muslems*, an evangelistic book written in English and Arabic[12] and designed entirely for Muslim readers.[13]

But most compelling is Salim's vision for his college. Here with his faculty he hopes to train Christian leaders who will forge a new future in which the church plays an active role in reconciliation. "Here we can deal with the political issues, the social issues, that trouble us. Palestinians who study in the States simply don't have this opportunity."[14] In addition to the usual courses in biblical studies and theology, the curriculum includes the history of the church (which does not exclude the place of Arab Christianity), the role of distinctive Middle Eastern churches (such as Eastern Orthodoxy), and the character of Palestinian culture.

Salim is working to develop a theological curriculum that meets the unique needs of the Palestinian pastor or lay leader. A critical debate on campus is how Christians should respond to violence. "This is the hottest issue we have," Salim affirms. Related pastoral themes likewise drive the curriculum. For instance, seminars are taught in the Women's Studies Program entitled "Having Your Husband in Prison." Laura Khoury, a popular young professor, teaches courses that help families through the adjustment of having a husband or son return home after months of trauma, torture, and stress. "The community wants to make him a hero—to promote his imprisonment, to give him honor." The young man, on the other hand, simply wants to live quietly, to heal, to integrate back into life.

Salim's vision for the church goes further. He believes that Jesus Christ came not just to reconcile humanity to God, but also to reconcile humanity to itself. In 1990 he founded Musalaha (Arabic, meaning "reconciliation"). This is a ministry designed to sponsor seminars and publish books that promote reconciliation grounded in biblical events of forgiveness such as

Jacob and Esau or Paul and Barnabas. Arab and Jewish believers should find the motive and model for forgiveness within their own Scriptures, and this is an excellent place to begin. But, as Salim argues, "only Christ can be the reconciler . . . between humanity and itself."[15] This is not an effort just to find common ground among Jews, Muslims, and Christians. This is cutting-edge evangelism in its most creative form, which speaks to the deepest pain inside the Middle Eastern world.

HANAN ASHRAWI, RAMALLAH, PROFESSOR, POLITICAL ACTIVIST

Many Americans today can quickly recognize a photograph of Hanan Ashrawi. The same is true in almost any Palestinian village. Simply to mention her name is to win broad smiles among Palestinian children and adults alike. In just a handful of years she has become a new heroine, a symbol of the new Palestinian leadership—well educated, articulate, and pragmatic. Her public recognition began in 1988 when she did the first of many interviews on ABC's "Nightline." As one of the leaders of the Palestinian negotiating team in Madrid in 1991, she met regularly with Secretary of State James Baker as he sought to forge a lasting peace in the Middle East. Hanan has become a leading voice for all Palestinians (Christian and Muslim) as her impeccable English and her powerful demeanor have won her success after success in grueling press conferences and interviews on every American television network. In debates, as the *Washington Post* put it, Hanan "takes no prisoners."[16]

I first met Hanan in a tent at East Jerusalem's Red Cross Center in May 1990, when she was on a hunger strike with about forty other Palestinian leaders. Then I interviewed her two years later in her home after her reputation had catapulted her into the limelight. Even as a young girl Hanan was well-known for being opinionated. Her sister, Nadia Abboushi, says, "Hanan grasped subjects passionately and could argue them with force."[17]

It surprised no one when Hanan earned a Ph.D. in medieval literature from the University of Virginia. As a professor of English at Bir Zeit University (Ramallah), she saw in literature the vehicle that could express injustice and promulgate change. Soon she found herself involved with students and leaders of the Palestinian liberation movements. She is even known for writing poetry, passionate poetry, that expresses the grief and anguish of her people.[18] While at Bir Zeit she has dodged bullets on campus and has seen four of her students killed in clashes with Israeli soldiers.

Hanan lives with her husband Emile and her two daughters, Zeina and Amal, across the street from an Israeli military prison in Ramallah. She jokes about the irony of her address since, she is convinced, the army watches her closely. "This way they only have to walk across the street to arrest me!" In fact, the army was not going to let her attend the 1991 peace conferences, and she would have been absent were it not for the intervention of Secretary of State Baker.

Few realize that Hanan comes from the Palestinian Christian community and is a member of the Anglican (Episcopal) Church. When reporters express surprise at this, her impatience boils over. "I am a Palestinian Christian, and I know what Christianity is. I am a descendant of the first Christians in the world, and Jesus Christ was born in my country, in my land. Bethlehem is a Palestinian town."[19] Even though she attended a Quaker high school in Ramallah, Hanan is not active in her church and quickly admits that promoting the Christian faith "is not central to [her] work."[20] Nevertheless, the values found in her schooling and in her family lend shape to her work today. For her, the church has not successfully worked for justice and change, thus it has lost credibility. Still, however, she believes that human rights must be grounded in personal faith.

When Hanan talks about the American church and the role it plays in the Middle East, her anguish is great. She even becomes angry. For her, Christian Zionists like the leaders at the International Christian Embassy "are more racist than the Israelis since they promote hate and division."[21] Above all, American evangelicals must beware of supporting Israel with zeal while lacking "humility, tolerance, and recognizing the humanity of others." "Sometimes," she says, "American Christians simply are not merciful."[22]

RIAH ABU EL-ASSAL, NAZARETH, PASTOR

Because Riah's family was in Lebanon when Israel declared its statehood in 1948, they were refused the right to return to their hometown of Nazareth even though Riah's father could prove that he was in Beirut on business with a British company. In 1949 the twelve-year-old Riah crossed the border illegally on foot with the consent of his parents and lived with an aunt in Nazareth for four years. In 1953 his four sisters and mother made the illegal return home. A serious battle began as the Israelis tried to expel them, but Riah's family won, proving that they had not emigrated to Lebanon in the first place and that their historic family home was in Nazareth. Five years later (1958) his father came home too.

"Abu El-Assal" means "father of honey"—which describes the traditional family business of beekeeping. But this was not to be Riah's future. Since he was born into an Episcopalian family, Riah grew up with the large Arab Christian community of Nazareth. He attended Anglican, Baptist, and even Greek Orthodox schools as a child. College found him traveling to India (Bishop's College, Calcutta), and he did his post-graduate studies in Geneva, Switzerland, and at the Near East School of Theology in Beirut, Lebanon. In 1966 he was ordained as a priest in the Episcopal Church. Since then his ministry has primarily been in churches in the cities of Haifa and Nazareth, and in Galilee. He has even served as a lecturer in Islamics (St. George's College, Jerusalem) and as the director of a home for the handicapped. Today he is priest of Christ Church, Nazareth, and archdeacon of the Diocese of Jerusalem.

This articulate, passionate leader has distinguished himself among the Palestinian clergy because he has felt called to integrate into the political mainstream of Israel, making a case for Arab justice. Since Riah is an Israeli citizen,[23] he even ran for a seat in the Knesset (the national Parliament) in 1984 and again in 1988. Even though his election bids failed, still, he likes to dream. "Imagine," he says, "if I had won. Every Knesset member gets to speak, and his words are permanently recorded in the Knesset record." I once asked him what he would say his first time at the microphone. "I would recite the words of Jesus!

Perhaps the Sermon on the Mount! Imagine! Jesus' words written into the Israeli Knesset records for the first time!"[24]

Riah's political activities, however, have brought him sharp criticism from both clergy colleagues and laity. The troubling question is whether a priest should be involved in politics at all. Riah has no doubts. He likes to cite stories from the Gospels to show how savvy Jesus was when it came to politics and justice.[25] Protecting his people—his flock—is a native instinct for Riah, and so he has been eager to enlist the support of any who would work with him. He has been active in the World Council of Churches and in 1985 joined a delegation of three Jews and three Arabs to meet Yasir Arafat in Tunis. His aim was to promote peace talks, but the price tag was high: the Israelis banned him from traveling out of the country for forty-two months.

Riah's quest for peace has taken him from meetings with Desmond Tutu to speaking engagements in Korea, Norway, Germany, Switzerland, Australia, Denmark, and the United States. He is a formidable leader with whom the Israelis must contend as they study the landscape of Palestinian intellectuals.

Despite all of his political activity, there is one mission that remains at the heart of this man's life. He is a pastor. He loves his people and serves them with his entire life. In Nazareth his church is well-known for its vitality and its caring ministries. But since his people are affected—truly affected—by the world of politics, he feels obliged to stand with them in that arena too.

AUDEH RANTISI, RAMALLAH, PASTOR, SCHOOL ADMINISTRATOR

Near the end of Al Tireh Street, Ramallah's main boulevard, visitors will see the impressive building of The Evangelical Boys' School, a school founded and administrated by Audeh Rantisi. His passion for the children of Ramallah no doubt comes from his own personal story: in July 1948, as a child of eleven, he joined his family as they were driven from their home in Lydda, near Tel Aviv. For three days they stumbled into the hills near Ramallah as refugees, with Israeli soldiers firing over their heads to keep them moving. At one point the young Audeh was nearly shot, but the bullet instead killed a nearby donkey. He was even lost among the refugees but later found his parents again. They traveled for twenty miles up mountains and down valleys without provisions until other Arabs escorted them to Ramallah. Clearly, those early memories never left the young man, and today the scars remain.[26]

Audeh's family had owned an expansive estate in Lydda and could trace their history there as far back as 1,600 years. Respected as manufacturers of olive oil soap, they enjoyed the esteem of their community. But now, in 1948, they were refugees, living in tents. To stay alive Audeh sold things on the street—from kerosene to cakes baked by his mother. But then when he was fifteen, nothing short of a miracle happened. An American businessman from Muskegon, Michigan, sold his business and opened a boarding school for Palestinians. Audeh was invited to enroll in "The Home of the Sons," and with extra effort, graduated from high school three years later. The generosity of still others brought him to The Bible College of Wales (Swansea in South Wales) and Aurora College in Illinois. After further study and two years as a missionary in Sudan, Audeh felt that he was being called to be a minister. He was ordained in the Episcopalian Church in 1968.

The common thread that runs through this remarkable man's life is his vision for children. Perhaps he still sees with his inner eye his own childhood, roughed up by the politics of another decade. He sees a young boy without a future and without hope rescued by a simple Christian opening a school and inviting him in. In 1965 he decided to begin his own school with just twelve boys in residence. By 1970 there were thirty boys. In 1974 he purchased land for a campus in faith. And in 1982 he began construction of the facility which sparkles in Ramallah today. It is so well known that any Arab taxi driver in Ramallah can take you there. Just say, "Audeh Rantisi," or "Evangelical School," and soon you will be at the front gate.

The cornerstone of The Evangelical Home for Boys reads: THIS BUILDING WAS BUILT TO THE GLORY OF GOD. UNLESS THE LORD BUILDS THE HOUSE, THOSE WHO BUILD IT LABOR IN VAIN. PS. 127:1. Nowhere in Palestine is such a mission more successfully carried out. Helped by organizations like Oxfam (England), the Mennonite Central Committee, and World Vision International, as well as an army of contributors from around the world, the school is a vibrant evangelical place of learning where everything from English and mathematics to electronics and computers is studied. A full gymnasium was completed just this year, and work has now begun on what will prove to be one of the finest libraries in Ramallah.

Audeh and his wife, Pat, have worked hard year after year, often overcoming incredible obstacles, to make this Christian school a reality. But their ministry goes further. They have become "bridge builders" to the Western church. Pat's gift of hospitality and Audeh's ready friendship have resulted in countless American and European volunteers and visitors coming through the school. It is not unusual to sit in their living room, hear the phone ring, and overhear Audeh talking and laughing with friends in Chicago or London or Paris or Cairo. More than once a late-night knock at their door has produced wearied, lost travelers who have come to meet "Audeh and Pat" and witness some of the "living stones" of Palestine. Earl Grey tea, biscuits, and a warm bed soon are theirs, and the next morning they will discover one of the little miracles of Palestine.

NOTES

1. Grand Rapids: Zondervan, 1990.
2. Israel insisted that the labels either say, "Made in Israel" (which was offensive to Mattin) or "Made in Ramallah" (which was meaningless in European and American markets.
3. Selwa comes from a remarkable family. Not only was her father in the clergy, but her mother, Cedar, works for the national YWCA in Jerusalem.
4. Personal interview, March 25, 1992.
5. Fortress Press will publish Mitri's important study about the history of the Middle Eastern church this year. His doctoral dissertation on the Palestinian Lutheran Church in Jordan was published in Germany in 1990 (Gütersloh).
6. Personal interview, March 31, 1992.
7. Al Haq does not, however, represent clients in court. Their research materials are simply used in court.
8. Personal interview, April 4, 1992.

9. Ibid.

10. The Intifada Gardens did not stop, however. Underground networks developed quickly to supply seeds and other needed materials.

11. Jad learned English both in England and the United States. His masters is from Rutgers University and his Ph.D. is from the University of East Anglia, United Kingdom.

12. Pasadena: Mandate Press, 1989.

13. This was written with Phil Gobel.

14. Personal interview, April 1, 1992.

15. *Musalah* promotional brochure, 3.

16. The *Washington Post*, November 4, 1991, D1. Hanan has been so successful with the Western media that one frustrated Israeli writer lamented, "Where is Yasir Arafat when we need him most!"

17. Personal interview, March 24, 1992.

18. A sample of her poetry is provided in the appendix.

19. The *Washington Post*, November 4, 1991, D1. *People* magazine wrote a personal profile of Hanan in its March 9, 1992, issue. She was also featured in *Time* in 1992 with a similar full-length profile.

20. Personal interview, March 25, 1992.

21. Ibid.

22. Ibid.

23. Palestinians living within the 1948 borders of Israel had the option of becoming Israeli citizens, a choice which today brings considerable advantages. The same option is not open to Arab residents of the West Bank and Gaza. Nazareth, Riah's home, is within "1948 Israel."

24. Personal interview, March 25, 1992.

25. For instance, citing Jesus' words, "Tell Herod, *that fox . . . ,*" Riah contends that Jesus never said "fox" in the original Aramaic. "Fox" is not a Middle Eastern title. Jesus may have said, "Tell Herod, *that dog . . . ,*" which conveys the passion and culture behind Luke 13:32. (*Emphasis mine.*)

26. The full story of Audeh Rantisi's experience has been published as *Blessed are the Peacemakers. A Palestinian Christian in the Occupied West Bank* (Grand Rapids: Zondervan, 1990). For these early years see pp. 23–39. See also M. C. King, *The Palestinians and the Churches, Vol. 1: 1948–1956* (Geneva: World Council of Churches, 1981).

Chapter Ten

EVANGELICALS AND THE LAND

"I feel that the destiny of the State of Israel is without question the most crucial international matter facing the world today. I believe that the people of Israel have not only a theological but also a historical and legal right to the land. I personally am Zionist, having gained that perspective from my belief in the Old Testament scriptures." (Jerry Falwell, cited in M. Simon, *Jerry Falwell and the Jews*, 62)[1]

"Assuming the validity of the ancient Promise of the Land and acknowledging Israel's security needs, are these enough to justify taking land that has been occupied by the Arabs for hundreds of years, or taking land that was 100% Arab in population? Do those factors justify flouting the principles of justice and mercy?" (Wesley G. Pippert, *Land of Promise, Land of Strife*, 124)[2]

The headlines of the *Jerusalem Post* for Monday, March 23, 1992, announced boldly: "American Evangelicals Pledge Support." On Sunday (the day before) more than eight hundred American evangelicals attended the International Christian Player Breakfast in Jerusalem ostensibly to "pray for the peace of Jerusalem" as commanded in Psalm 122. But as so often happens in Israel, religion and politics became one. With Jerusalem's mayor, Teddy Kollek, joining him at the platform, Prime Minister Yitzhaq Shamir spoke to the crowd and received three standing ovations. His speech was interrupted countless times by applause. Pastors, business persons, and politicians were all there affirming their support for Israel as evangelicals.

But the agenda was more strategic than this. In an American election year when Israel's request for a $10 billion loan guarantee was being debated, the conference brochure made their purposes explicit: "We Christians call upon our Bible-believing brothers and sisters to re-examine their political support and not vote for any presidential candidate, prime minister, or other politician whose policy concerning Israel would be contrary to the mandates of God."

After the breakfast, everyone was asked to walk to the Western Wall, where speakers urged the crowd to vote only for those candidates who would support the loan guarantees and to defeat any presidential candidate who would offer land or autonomy to the Palestinians.

As the *Jerusalem Post* reporter listened to it, this was the voice of America's 80 million evangelicals speaking.

On the next day the organizers of the breakfast launched a Bible-reading marathon on the Mount of Olives. Nine hundred people each read fifteen to thirty minutes to complete the entire Bible. It was a "prophetic event," they announced, fulfilling Isaiah 2, "The word of God shall go forth out of Jerusalem." Again the Israelis looked on, took notes, and witnessed more evidence of American evangelicals standing in solidarity with Israel's national purposes.

It is a curious fact of history that original support for Israel's nationhood in the 1940s and 1950s came from liberal Protestant Christians in the United States.[3] After witnessing the tragedy of the Jewish holocaust, it made sense to support a people seeking a refuge from persecution. In fact, in 1939 when 83 percent of the American population opposed the admission of European refugees (including Jews), the Presbyterian Church petitioned the government aggressively to let them in. In May 1939, the General Assembly condemned Nazism, committed itself to rescuing European Jewry, and vowed to fight against anti-Semitism in the United States. In 1940 it even urged congregations to give sanctuary to fleeing refugees.

But these same mainline Protestant churches began to

express outspoken criticism after Israel's 1967 war. Israel's expansionist policies and abuses to Palestinians seemed to be an affront to the very values Judaism sought and could not find in Europe. Today Presbyterians, Methodists, Episcopalians, and others have lodged harsh complaints. Publications such as *The Link* (published by Americans for Middle East Understanding) often host authors from these churches who write critical essays on Israel.[4] For instance, the January/March 1992 issue devoted eleven pages to Paul Hopkins, secretary for the Middle East (Presbyterian Church, U.S.A.) from 1980 to 1985. When Hopkins began to speak out about Palestinian concerns based on his own numerous experiences, he was charged with being "anti-Semitic." This lengthy essay was his defense.

Since 1967 evangelicals have taken the forefront in support of Israel. Yet the same shift I described among mainline churches is now at work even within this community. Evangelicals in surprising numbers are "crossing the line" and witnessing firsthand the nature of life in the West Bank. Palestinian pastors are writing and speaking, and in the last few years, their voices have been heard.

THE BASIS OF EVANGELICAL SUPPORT FOR ISRAEL

To be fair, the vast majority of evangelicals instinctively believe that vigorous support for Israel is the only appropriate response to the conflicts in the Middle East. It has little to do with history, less to do with politics. Evangelical commitment to Israel is grounded in sincere Christian conviction. The average believer in the pew is persuaded that such support is God's will: the Jews are God's people, and they are returning to the land God promised to them. As someone said to me recently, "You just can't get around it. The Jews are chosen. And this means they get special treatment."

Because evangelicals have always had a passionate commitment to theology and the Bible, two theological themes that come from the Scriptures have influenced their view.

Dispensationalism. First, many evangelicals are *dispensationalists.* Even those who do not use this title or understand it still follow an informal dispensational theology when they study the Scriptures. They divide biblical history into a number of historic periods (such as the era before the fall of Adam, the period after the giving of the Law, and the "dispensation" of the church age). Dispensationalists examine each period, carefully studying the methods of God's efforts among his people. Many are familiar with *The Scofield Reference Bible*, which applies the dispensational scheme in comments throughout the text of the Scriptures.

Most dispensationalists distinguish God's program for the church from God's program for Israel. As Charles Ryrie, a noted dispensationalist, puts it, "The church did not begin in the Old Testament but on the day of Pentecost, and the church is not presently fulfilling promises made to Israel in the Old Testament that have not yet been fulfilled."[5] This means that the church is a separate entity from Israel, living on a parallel track, possessing a different covenant. Therefore there is no interference between the biblical Israelites and modern Israel. A straight line can be drawn between them, and the Christian church will not merge with Israel until the end of the age.

The conclusion of this point of view is simple: If the church does not supplant Israel and if Christians are not the new children of Abraham, then the promises of Abraham appropriately belong to modern Israel even today. Authors will frequently presuppose this deduction when they describe the building of the state of Israel. Listen, for instance, to the words of John Walvoord of Dallas Seminary: "The repossession of a portion of their ancient land by the new state of Israel is especially striking because of the promise given by God to Abraham of perpetual title to the land between Egypt and the Euphrates."[6]

Walvoord clearly believes that the politics of modern-day Israel are a continuation of the politics of Old Testament Israel. The taking of land is justified for biblical reasons.

Other interpreters disagree heartily. Their view is that God has worked consistently with people throughout biblical history, and the people of God form a continuity from Adam and Noah to the early church. There are not today two people of God with different programs. In each era God has presented himself in the same way, and those who acknowledge his grace in faith are his people. Thus gentile Christians stand on a par with Jewish believers and can read the Old Testament as belonging to them. And today there are not "two Israels"—a natural Israel (the Jews) and a spiritual Israel (the church). Pointing to passages like Ephesians 2:14–17, they affirm that God has abolished in Christ categories that formerly divided. God has one people: those who follow his Son.

Eschatology[7]. An important second dimension to this discussion is that many evangelicals are persuaded that Israel is playing a role in the end times. In 1948 when the fledgling Israeli state was established, prophecy was fulfilled. Listen again to the words of Walvoord:

> Of the many peculiar phenomena which characterize the present generation, few events can claim equal significance as far as Biblical prophecy is concerned with that of the return of Israel to their land. It constitutes a preparation for the end of the age, the setting for the coming of the Lord for His church, and the fulfillment of Israel's prophetic destiny.[8]

There is no doubt that one book played a leading role in popularizing this understanding of Middle Eastern history and the Bible. Hal Lindsey's *Late Great Planet Earth* (published in 1970) was a spellbinding description of the fulfillment of prophecy and the imminent end of the world. I still remember reading it for the first time in 1972 while I was living in the Middle East as a college student. I was twenty, and it disturbed me to no end! At least, I reasoned, if the end of the world was coming, I was in the perfect spot to watch it happen! Lindsey's book is still popular today and has sold a record-breaking 25 million copies.[9]

This view is also called "premillennialist" because it designs a special pattern for the unfolding of the end. Before Christ returns to establish a thousand-year reign (the Millennium), certain prophecies must be fulfilled. In other words, there is a prophetic prelude to Christ's return and rule (hence "premillennialism," or Christ's premillennial return). There will be divinely decreed signs such as earthquakes, famines, wars, the appearance of the Antichrist, and the preaching of the gospel to all nations. Prominent among these signs is the restoration of Israel to the land. This event alone starts the "eschatological timeclock"—it lights the fuse that will detonate Armageddon, the great catastrophic war which Christ will end with his second coming. Lindsey calls the restoration of national Israel "the key to the jigsaw puzzle": "With the Jewish nation reborn in the land of Palestine, ancient Jerusalem once again under total Jewish control for the first time in 2600 years, and talk of rebuilding the great Temple, the most important prophetic sign of Jesus Christ's soon coming is before us."[10]

Together these two themes—a dispensational commitment to Israel's separate existence and an eschatological interest in fulfilled prophecy—have built the bedrock of evangelical attitudes toward the Middle East. Evangelicals are quick to say that a literal reading of the Bible and a sincere appreciation of the miracle of Israel's restoration in the twentieth century ought to be enough to convince any skeptic. But most important, this commitment should be translated into political support for Israel. Thus on January 27, 1992, a full-page ad in the *Washington Times* announced boldly, "Seventy Million Christians Urge President Bush to Approve Loan Guarantees for Israel." Under the ad thirty-three Christian leaders listed their names explaining, "We deeply believe in the biblical prophetic vision of the ingathering of exiles to Israel, a miracle we are now seeing fulfilled." Who are the 70 million? The ad is clear: they are America's evangelicals. Many evangelicals like myself, however, take deep offense at advertisements such as this, which pretend to speak for the entire evangelical community in a secular forum. They do not.

CHRISTIAN ZIONISM AND THE CHRISTIAN EMBASSY, JERUSALEM

This unqualified endorsement of Israel's politics based on biblical principles has spawned a movement called Christian Zionism. They have utterly wed religious conviction with political realities and interpreted biblical faithfulness in terms of fidelity to Israel's future. And the Israeli government loves it. In 1980 Jerry Falwell received from Prime Minister Menachem Begin the Jabotinsky Award for Service to the Cause of Israel.

The award did not recognize Falwell's merits as a Christian minister, but his efforts to assist Israel politically.

Christian Zionists have a zeal for Israel and are willing to promote more or less political agendas. Therefore it comes as no surprise that numerous organizations have grown up with important offices in Israel: the list includes Bridges for Peace, The International Christian Embassy, Friends of Jerusalem, Christian Friends of Israel, Israel Vistas, The National Christian Leadership Conference for Israel, and Christian's Israel Public Action Campaign. Together they raise millions of dollars in aid for Israel, sponsor conferences both in the United States and in Israel, distribute vast quantities of literature, and promote tours for Christian pilgrims.[11]

Take one example. The International Christian Embassy is located on a quiet street in West Jerusalem. Founded in 1980, its mission is to express to Israel heartfelt support for its life and future, to "comfort Zion" as Isaiah 40:1 says. Believing that the restoration of Israel fulfills important biblical prophecies, the embassy teaches that the "destiny" of nations and even individual Christians is determined by their attitude toward this new country.[12] As their director once told me, "Christians will be judged by how they treat Israel."[13] To neglect Israel and its restoration is to incur judgment and to miss God's blessing in what appears to be "the last days."

On my visits to the embassy I have always been impressed with their friendliness and eagerness to enlist my support—and disturbed by their political involvements. Their promotional brochures feature photographs and endorsements from former Prime Minister Menachem Begin, Jerusalem Mayor Teddy Kollek, and Prime Minister Yitzhak Shamir. Their literature table sells books and videos produced by the Israeli army. And yet in the midst of these efforts there is no interest in carrying on a ministry to Judaism like Paul's—a ministry that proclaims Jesus as Messiah. In fact, the embassy intentionally avoids any discussion of this "divisive subject."[14]

Each year the embassy promotes what has become its most public effort of all: the Christian celebration of the Feast of Tabernacles. Thousands of Christians from numerous countries pack into Jerusalem to join in the festivities. Political speeches are given by Israeli leaders, and affirmations of support are proclaimed.

Perhaps the most troubling thing about the embassy is its overt antagonism toward the Palestinian people. Its leaders readily deny the validity of Palestinian Christianity[15] and compare the spirit of the Arab resistance movement with the "spirit found in the holocaust."[16] As one embassy leader said to me, the Intifada is another form of Nazism.

On an earlier occasion, the embassy director stereotyped all Arabs as untrustworthy. My questions pressed the point: "Should we not care for the Palestinian Christian community too?"

The answer was stunning: "They are not really as Christian as you might think." The word *Arab* came out as if it were unclean. "Arabs lie, they cheat in business deals, and they will give you their word one day and then deny it. They don't seem to respect life or truth like anyone else does."

I was stunned at his words. "But don't the Palestinians have rights?" I pressed.

"Sometimes," he said, "you have to keep God's long-term plan in mind. Sometimes particular rights have to be suspended."

I decided to try another approach. "Do you know any moderate Arabs worth listening to?"

He said quickly, "After ten years here, no."[17]

Needless to say, I left the embassy that day deeply troubled.

Fortunately there are more reasonable voices among the Christian Zionists. Bridges for Peace is directed by Clarence Wagner and is the oldest Christian Zionist work in Israel.[18] It has an impressive newspaper called *Dispatch from Jerusalem*,[19] which monitors political and religious developments between the United States and Israel. Their second publication, *Jerusalem Prayer Letter*, is far more contentious. In addition to helpful explanations of the Jewish traditions, it frequently lapses into hard-sell polemics, insisting that true Christians give unlimited political support to Israel.

Bridges for Peace does just what its name implies. It builds bridges, particularly between the Jewish and the Christian communities. "Opening Doors" is a program that can place Christian visitors to Israel in Israeli homes.[20] "Operation Ezra" works to assist Israeli poor and especially the new Russian immigrants.[21]

Curiously, there is no planned ministry to Christian Arabs, much less to the Palestinians as a whole. No bridges are being built. And American visitors who come to the country through the direction of the Christian Zionist organizations can spend weeks in Israel/Palestine and not realize that there is a whole other community (the Palestinian community) that is being overlooked.

A NEW EVANGELICAL OUTLOOK

Many of us within the evangelical church are offended by Christian Zionism. While we are committed to peace and justice for all parties in Israel/Palestine, we are offended by those people whose faith is consumed by the politics of Israel's restoration. It is presumptuous for the Christian Embassy to be called an "embassy" at all.[22] In its literature it compares itself with foreign embassies that have "forsaken" Jerusalem and moved to Tel Aviv. Worse still, it is courted by leading Israeli politicians, especially in the conservative Likud Party, who see these Christians advancing their political aims. But the "embassy" bears no diplomatic mission for all of the West's churches. It does not come close. No evangelical majority has asked the embassy to represent it.

Christianity Today published a contemporary study of Christian Zionism in its March 9, 1992, issue and there recorded the growing criticisms of the movement from within evangelicalism itself. The question is whether such Zionists represent the spirit of political nationalism more than the Spirit of Christ. The magazine also analyzed the sweeping changes that evangelicals are making in their thinking. Israel must, according to the average believer, stand at the bar of international justice and human rights.

Professor Marvin Wilson is a specialist on Judaism and teaches at Gordon College, an evangelical institution near Boston. His words sum up the new outlook accurately: "The number one obstacle to peace is nationalism, because so often it insists on the denial of the other guy. A biblical view can't be anti-Arab and pro-Israel, or anti-Israel and pro-Arab. God's heart is where justice is."[23]

Numerous evangelical authors have likewise turned their attention to the problem of Israel/Palestine in a new way. As far back as 1970 Frank Epp wrote *Whose Land Is Palestine?* exploring the political crisis with genuine balance.[24] In 1988 Wesley Pippert, a correspondent for United Press International, wrote one of the best books yet released on the subject from an evangelical perspective.[25] Even Multnomah Press has released a new volume that gives genuine respect for Palestinian rights. It's author, Stanley Ellisen, concludes that Israel should be treated like any other secular state in the world, giving it both security considerations and expecting from it appropriate human rights.[26]

Today evangelicals are beginning to experience a shift in focus. In a poll conducted by *Christianity Today* in 1992, 39 percent of the magazine's readers said that their view of Israel was "more critical" than before. Eighty-eight percent believe "Christians should hold the State of Israel to the same standard of justice and human rights in its international affairs and internal affairs as any other nation." Convinced that biblical teachings about justice are equally important to prophecies of the end, they are looking for new ways to understand God's will in the Middle East.

EVANGELICALS FOR MIDDLE EAST UNDERSTANDING (EMEU)

Many evangelicals are making sincere overtures to the Palestinian Christian churches directly. In 1985 Dr. Ray Bakke and Dr. Don Wagner traveled to Cyprus, Syria, Jordan, Israel/Palestine, and Egypt on a three-week "listening tour" coordinated by the Middle East Council of Churches.[27] They came away with four conclusions: (1) The crisis in the Middle East demands increased moral and spiritual support from Western Christians; (2) Christian Zionists represent a danger-ous dynamic in the volatile Middle East as they give uncondi-tional monetary and political support to Israel while ignoring the Arabs; (3) Western Christians know virtually nothing about the rich legacy of Arab history; (4) Western evangelicals are involved in excellent ministries throughout the Middle East. They have demonstrated keen sensitivity to the issues of the region and have begun to form a partnership with Middle East Christians.[28]

Arab Christians asked Bakke and Wagner to help them address these issues in the West. While progress had been made with Catholics and mainline churches, few evangelicals understood the concerns of the Palestinian Christians.

In 1986 twenty-five Christian leaders from the Middle East, North America, and England met under the leadership of John Stott. In addition, representatives from InterVarsity Christian Fellowship, the Middle East Council of Churches, the Lausanne Committee for World Evangelization, the Anglican Church, the National Council of Churches (USA), and many others were present. As a result, Evangelicals for Middle East Understanding was born. Today it has over a thousand supporters on its mailing list.

Ray Bakke, the chairman of EMEU is clear that his organization is not "anti-Jew" or "against the state of Israel." Christians should not, he believes, support an intolerable nationalism that oppresses people. EMEU works to inform American Christians within the evangelical camp about the realities of life in Israel/Palestine and the suffering of fellow Christians there.

Each autumn EMEU and the Middle East Council of Churches sponsors a conference on Cyprus, where Arab pastors and evangelicals from America and Europe can meet. In 1991, 150 Christian leaders met: 90 from the West and 60 from Middle Eastern countries.[29] Representatives from the ancient Middle Eastern churches (Coptic, Melkite, Orthodox, Catholic) join with more recent Arab denominations (Lutheran, Baptist, Anglican, etc.) to explain the plight of their people and their needs as Christian leaders. For the hundreds of pastors who have attended, the conference is an unforgettable experience.[30]

Don Wagner, a cofounder of EMEU, has also formed his own ministry, Mercy Corps, in Chicago. In addition to disseminating information about Israel/Palestine, Wagner organizes trips to Israel for evangelicals who wish to see "the other side of the issue." Through his contacts with the Middle East Council of Churches, Wagner has led countless pastors "behind the scenes" from Galilee to Gaza, letting the Palestinian people speak for themselves.[31]

The change in evangelical attitudes has even been noted by Middle East "watchers" outside the evangelical mainstream. *The Link* is a quarterly journal published by Americans for Middle East Understanding.[32] Its entire October/November 1992 issue was devoted to a study of changing evangelical attitudes. In an interview in its pages, Dr. John Stott, a leading evangelical spokesperson, was asked, "What is your perspective on Zionism and Christian Zionism?" He replied, "After considerable study, I have concluded that Zionism and especially Christian Zionism are Biblically untenable."[33]

From 1979 to 1981 Christian leaders met regularly in LaGrange, Illinois, to establish a theological consensus on the Israel/Palestine issue. Eventually "The Lagrange Declarations I and II" were endorsed, published in the pages of *Sojourner's Magazine*, and signed by more than five thousand U.S. Christians.[34] Its signatories came from all parts of the church, including many leading evangelicals: Jim Wallis (*Sojourners*), Nicholas Woltersdorff (Calvin College), Paul Rees (World Vision), John Alexander and Mark Olsen (*The Other Side*), Bill Star (Young Life), Walden Howard (Faith at Work), and Bruce Birch and Dewey Beegle (Wesley Seminary) just to name a few.

The declaration calls for a new sensitivity and a new commitment to biblical justice in the Holy Land:

> As believers committed to Christ and his Kingdom, we challenge the popular assumptions about biblical interpretation and the presuppositions of political loyalty held so widely by fellow Christians in their attitudes toward conflict in the Middle East. We address this urgent call to the church of Jesus Christ to hear and heed those voices crying out as bruised reeds for justice in the land where our Lord walked, taught, was crucified, and rose from the dead. We have closed our hearts to these voices and isolated ourselves even from the pleading of low Christians who continue to live in that land.

Forthrightly, we declare our conviction that in the process of establishing the state of Israel, a deep injustice was done to the Palestinian people, confiscating their land and driving many into exile and even death. Moreover, for 13 years, large portions of the holy land and its people, including the West Bank of the Jordan River, Gaza, and East Jerusalem, have suffered under foreign military occupation, even as in our Lord's time. . . . We confess our silence, our indifference, our hard-heartedness, and our cowardice, all too often, in the face of these dehumanizing realities.[35]

SUMMARY

I have been converted by experiences and study. As an evangelical brought up on sermons and books explaining the chosenness of Israel in God's plan for history, I am now persuaded that the church cannot be entangled in a political agenda in the Middle East that destroys people and pursues injustice. The Old Testament continually calls God's people to protect "the alien, the orphan, and the widow." The New Testament says that the purity of our faith must be seen in how we treat "the foreign neighbor" (Luke 10:25–37). The Palestinian is my neighbor. Many Palestinians are my Christian brothers and sisters.

If Israel makes biblical claims to statehood, Israel must be an exemplar of biblical righteousness among the nations. At the very least, Israel must be comparable to the other nations in moral conduct. And if comparable, then it should be held to the same standards of justice we expect from countries such as South Africa, where our criticisms have been harsh.

Some Christians who have expressed criticisms such as these have been accused of anti-Semitism. Evangelicals who stand opposed to the secular nationalism of Israel are not discriminating against Judaism as a people. On the contrary, evangelical critics are expressing dissatisfaction with the behavior of a nation that ought to know better—a nation whose possession of the Scriptures ought to give it more light. The prophets of the Old Testament, men like Isaiah and Jeremiah, loved Israel deeply. And yet this did not weaken their exhortations when Israel sinned.

I believe that evangelicals need to join these prophetic voices. It is because of Israel's rich spiritual heritage that she should become a light to the nations. It is because Israel has been abused in the past—exiled into foreign nations—that Israel must not be the abuser today.

Recently I spent an afternoon and evening walking through the back streets of Beit Sahour outside Bethlehem with a young Palestinian Christian named Inam Bonoura. Inam works as a secretary at Bethlehem Bible College, and she gave me hours of her time, not simply to give a tour of her village, but to share something of her own thoughts about her country.

Two things stood out as we talked. Inam told me about her one and only visit to the United States. She was on a bus traveling through Indiana, and suddenly after four hours it hit her: she had never gone so far in one direction in her life. Israel had restricted her freedom of movement so much that the geographical scope of her world was "less than four hours wide." She cried when she realized how expansive and free she felt that afternoon north of Indianapolis.

We talked at length about America, its virtues and shortcomings, its relationship to Israel, and the role of the Christian church. We stopped on the road alongside the biblical Shepherds' Fields, and as I looked up at Bethlehem on the horizon, I found myself unable to answer some of Inam's questions. "How can America, your America, that believes in freedom, support Israel when it acts like this?" Such questions are frequent in the Middle East and easy to explain to Palestinians: The United States isn't a perfect country. We make mistakes even among our allies.

Then came the bombshell: "But why do American *Christians* support the Israelis as well? Why don't they help us? Why not even us, the Palestinian Christians?" As we walked on, I discovered to my shame that I had no answer. But at least I am confident today that evangelicals everywhere in America are going to change that record.

NOTES

1. New York: Jonathan David, 1984.

2. Waco: Word, 1988.

3. R. Ruether and H. Ruether, *The Wrath of Jonah. The Crisis of Religious Nationalism in the Israeli-Palestinian Conflict* (Harper & Row, 1989), 173.

4. For information about *The Link,* write: Americans for Middle East Understanding, Inc., Room 241, 475 Riverside, Drive, New York, NY 10115. "AMEU" likewise offers many books for sale about the Israelis and Palestinians. Virtually all of their publications have a decidedly pro-Palestinian slant.

5. C. C. Ryrie, "Dispensation, Dispensationalism," in W. Elwell, ed., *The Evangelical Dictionary of Theology* (Grand Rapids: Baker, 1984), 322.

6. J. Walvoord, *The Nations, Israel and the Church in Prophecy,* three volumes in one (Grand Rapids: Zondervan, 1988), 2:25.

7. *Eschatology* means "the study of the end times." Thus it is common to read that modern Israel is playing *an eschatological role* in the twentieth century.

8. J. Walvoord, *The Nations, Israel and the Church in Prophecy,* 2:26.

9. In 1991 I read *The Late Great Planet Earth* carefully with a group of college seniors. They looked up every reference in the Bible and analyzed Lindsey's interpretation. I was surprised when they unanimously told me that it was one of the most unconvincing books they had ever read. As one student put it, "Lindsey simply bends the Scriptures to say what he wants."

10. H. Lindsey (with C. C. Carlson), *The Late Great Planet Earth* (Grand Rapids: Zondervan, 1970), 47.

11. For a survey see Ken Sidey, "For the Love of Zion," *Christianity Today* (March 9, 1992), 46–50.

12. International Christian Embassy, Jerusalem, promotional brochure "Prepare Ye the Way of the Lord," 4.

13. Johann Lückhoff, personal interview, March 30, 1992. He called "love for Israel" the first fruit of the Spirit in the Middle East.

14. Ibid.

15. Ibid. Lückhoff remarked that Naim Ateek, the Arab pastor of St. George's Episcopal Church, is an example of someone whose judgment is "clouded by Palestinian politics." On another occasion he denied that he had ever met any Arabs who were indeed Christians.

16. Jim Schultz, embassy staff member, personal interview, March 30, 1992.

17. Personal interview, 1989.

18. Bridges for Peace was founded in 1976 by G. Douglas Young.

19. Published at Bridges for Peace, Box 33145, Tulsa, OK 74153. Circulation: 35,000.

20. In March 1992 Bridges for Peace placed me for an evening in Settlement Beth El in the splendid home of Helen and Yehuda Borer. As promised, the evening was one of the most rewarding I have ever spent in Israel/Palestine.

21. Organizations such as Bridges for Peace do a great deal more, and this is only a summary. It commonly sponsors conferences in the United States such as one in June 1992, entitled "Israel and the Church: Past, Present, and Future."

22. Even Clarence Wagner, director of Bridges for Peace, expressed to me his dissatisfaction with the way the International Christian Embassy postures itself as "an embassy."

23. K. Sidey, "For the Love of Zion," *Christianity Today*, March 9, 1992, 50.

24. F. H. Epp, *Whose Land Is Palestine? The Middle East Problem in Perspective* (Grand Rapids: Eerdmans, 1970).

25. W. G. Pippert, *Land of Promise, Land of Strife. Israel at Forty* (Waco: Word, 1988).

26. S. A. Ellisen, *Who Owns the Land? The Arab-Israeli Conflict* (Portland: Multnomah, 1991).

27. The "MECC" is an ecumenical body uniting 8 million Arab Christians worldwide. Its American offices are located at Room 614, 475 Riverside Drive, New York, NY 10115.

28. R. Bakke, *International Urban Associates Newsletter* (Chicago, 1992).

29. See "The Other Peace Conference," *Christianity Today*, November, 11, 1991, 46–48.

30. Evangelicals for Middle East Understanding may be contacted at 847 Chicago Avenue, Suite 3C, Evanston, IL 60202. FAX (708) 733-0904. It publishes a newsletter called *Signs of Hope.*

31. Mercy Corps may be contacted at the same address as EMEU (note 30).

32. *The Link*, Rm. 241, 475 Riverside Drive, New York, NY 10115. FAX (212)-870-2050.

33. Ibid., 7.

34. *Sojourners*, July 1979.

35. See D. Wagner, "Beyond Armageddon," *The Link*, October/November 1992, 7.

EPILOGUE

"Come, let us go up to the mountain of the LORD,
    to the house of the God of Jacob;
that he may teach us his ways
    and that we may walk in his paths."
For out of Zion shall go forth instruction,
    and the word of the LORD from Jerusalem.
He shall judge between many peoples,
    and shall arbitrate between strong nations far away;
they shall beat their swords into plowshares,
    and their spears into pruning hooks;
nation shall not lift up sword against nation,
    neither shall they learn war any more;
but they shall all sit under their own vines and under their
own fig trees,
    and no one shall make them afraid;
    for the mouth of the LORD of hosts has spoken. (Mic.
4:2–4)

A couple of years ago an Israeli dentist was attending a professional conference in New York City. Seminars were being offered on dental research, techniques, and approaches to dentistry around the world. He was intrigued when he noted that another Israeli was on the seminar agenda, and so he attended with curiosity.

The seminar was about comparative enamel wear on the

teeth of people living in the Middle East and elsewhere in the world. The researcher had come to some startling discoveries: In Israel enamel loss through teeth grinding was astonishingly higher in Tel Aviv (his population sample) than in the Western world. In other words, Israelis (and we can assume Arabs too) are under so much stress, that teeth grinding has reached almost epidemic proportions! Once I was walking through the back streets of Tel Aviv late at night and had this astounding image of people everywhere in their beds grinding their teeth in their sleep!

No one is happy in Israel/Palestine. The Israelis are not happy. The Palestinians are not happy. Turmoil victimizes the emotions of anyone who must live in the country. I have had close friends who work in Jerusalem suffer nervous break-downs because of the stress. Others who serve the refugee camps experience surprising physical symptoms of what psychologists call "toxic anxiety." Israeli Jews in Chicago have confided to me that while they love Israel, they cannot bear the thought of making "that crazy place" their permanent home.

Israeli dissatisfaction with the status quo was exhibited fully on Tuesday, June 23, 1992, when the conservative Likud Party led by Yitzhak Shamir was summarily defeated. Likud has been antagonistic toward the peace process with the Arabs, and since the 1970s when it came to power, it has aggressively pursued the illegal settlement of the conquered West Bank.

For Israelis the defeat was a statement, a forceful statement, that the aggressive policies of Shamir had become intolerable. Henry Siegman, executive director of the American Jewish Congress, commented: "The election results constitute a repudiation of those who traded on Israel's very real security fears to advance narrow ideological goals."[1] What happened? According to exit polls, the hundreds of thousands of recent immigrants from the former Soviet Union voted for the more moderate Labor Party nearly three to one. And young Israelis, fatigued with the despair of conflict and increasing international criticism, likewise left the hawkish Likud camp in droves.

For Palestinians the election was a sign of hope. Israel's new prime minister, Yitzhak Rabin, is the leader of the Labor Party and is clearly committed to compromise on the question of occupied lands. Trading land for peace is a stated platform of his government. He advocated that the country shift its financial priorities from investment in settlement building to social and economic needs within the country.

ARE THINGS GETTING BETTER?

Some would say yes: the atmosphere is changing in Israel/Palestine. And as a sign of this they point to the current peace negotiations in Washington, D.C., continued by Rabin following the election. Remarkably, these talks among Israel, Lebanon, and Syria are even including indirect input from the Palestine Liberation Organization! While the PLO is certainly an organization that leaves a lot to be desired, still it is the Palestinian political body of choice among residents of the West Bank and Gaza.

Nevertheless, the Palestinians are cautious. They recall that the new Prime Minister Rabin himself was an aggressive antagonist once against the Intifada. *An Nahar*, an East Jerusalem Palestinian newspaper, recalls that when Rabin was defense minister he ordered illegal house demolitions and deportations as a means of putting down the uprising.[2] Even if the new government halts all of the settlements on the West Bank, that leaves unresolved the problem of settlements that exist already, settlements that have just begun, and land confiscated over the past twenty-five years. Will these be returned? Will financial reparations be made? Will West Bank communities gain democratic freedoms? These items will be negotiated passionately in the coming months.

These are months of opportunity in Israel. New national priorities are being fashioned, and all sides are watching closely to see what results. The other day I asked a young Palestinian recently returned from the West Bank city of Ramallah if there had been much street fighting this summer (1992). "No," he remarked, "everyone is watching to see if things are going to change; to see if the army will let go. The people are optimistic."

Yet severe conflicts remain on the back pages of the daily newspaper. Both Arabs and Israelis continue to witness breathtaking examples of violence. For instance, on one day in October 1992, Palestinians who were demonstrating in Jerusalem in solidarity with three thousand Arab prisoners on hunger strike were attacked by the army with tear gas and bullets. In one day, one Arab was killed and forty-seven others were wounded.[3] One week later a Palestinian bomb in a van in Tel Aviv killed one Israeli and seriously injured two others.[4] A close look at any major newspaper will disclose stories such as these on a regular basis.

The climate of Israeli/Palestinian political life has changed temporarily. There is a new openness, a new interest in looking for ways to compromise. Yet it would be wrong if American Christians concluded that the "problem" was over, that the Middle East was on the mend. The Intifada is simply exhausted, and so is the Israeli public. It is at moments like these that new voices have a chance to be heard. Therefore we must remain unflinching in our commitment to peace and justice in this tormented country. Other voices, voices of radicalism and violence (such as the Muslim Hamas and Islamic Jihad), are still eager to be heard and wait on the edges of Palestinian and Israeli society.

Yet fresh conflict is always just around the corner. On Thursday, December 17, 1992, the Israeli army expelled 415 Palestinian men from the country because an Israeli border guard had been kidnapped and killed. The men were accused of associating with radical political groups (allegedly responsible for the murder), given no trial, and simply placed on buses and deposited across the Lebanese border. Such expulsions are in strict violation of the Geneva Convention human rights guarantees, and the next day the United Nations Security Council formally condemned Israel. At once Gaza was placed under curfew, demonstrations erupted, and in the conflicts that followed, the army shot and killed six people (including an eight-year-old girl) and wounded thirty others as well.

Despite an international protest, on Monday, December 25 (Christmas), the Israeli Supreme Court upheld the expulsion by a five to two vote. On Tuesday, December 26, Lebanon announced that it was refusing the men entry to their country in order to force Israel's hand. Yitzak Rabin even refused to permit the International Red Cross to supply the men with aid, saying that "it would not be humanitarian. It would merely be political." As I write, these men still languish in southern Lebanon without sufficient food, clothing, or medicine. And the peace talks in Washington have nearly ceased.

Palestinian Christians likewise worry about the future. In the spring of 1993 they witnessed one more example of military intimidation. An ancient tradition on Easter each year is to carry light from the Church of the Holy Sepulchre in Jerusalem to worshippers waiting with candles throughout the country. It is a unifying and thrilling experience that Christian families happily anticipate. But in 1993, for the first time, the army disrupted the services in Jerusalem and confiscated everyone's candle. Even waiting worshippers in outlying towns such as Ramallah and Bethlehem were dispersed by the military.

In April 1993 the Israeli government took severe measures against the Palestinians on the West Bank and Gaza. Palestinians were prohibited from entering Israel under any circumstances. This keeps more than 100,000 Palestinians from going to their jobs and, as *Time* magazine reported, costs the Arabs 2.3 million dollars a day in lost wages. Closing off the West Bank and Gaza means that money, food, and medicine are now in short supply because even though the Palestinians cannot enter Israel, neither can they develop economic relations with other countries.

As Christians our interest in areas of world crisis change from year to year. One year it is the dissolving Soviet Union, another year it is the war in Yugoslavia or famine in Somalia. When the Israeli/Palestinian problem temporarily slips from the limelight, Palestinians fear that this will mean their loss. Without international pressure and criticism, they stand powerless against the well-organized Israeli government. Evangelicals therefore must remain diligent, like the prophet Ezekiel atop the towers of Jerusalem's walls. Without accountability, without worldwide scrutiny, the overtures for peace may come to nothing and the cycle of suffering only continues.

CHARGES OF ANTI-SEMITISM

I was surprised in May (1992) when I received a phone call from the Jewish Anti-Defamation League in New York City. An earlier draft of this book's first chapter was published as an article in a church journal, and much to my amazement it had been noted, catalogued, and found wanting among these leaders in New York. A rabbi phoned me at my office one afternoon and insisted that I clarify my viewpoints on Israel and Christian thought. The implication was clear: Criticism of Israel was intolerable. It was a subtle form of anti-Semitism. And I was being called to account.

Some who read this book will think the same thing. These pages report some very harsh events. They are critical of a political nation that makes religious, spiritual claims to justify its existence. Is Israel exempt from these criticisms? Is it wrong to lodge criticisms when we are talking about people with biblical ancestry?

One night recently I happened to be in Jerusalem during Pentecost and decided that since this was a holy season, it might be good to wander down to the temple site and see what was going on. I stood in the Western Wall promenade for a while and then wandered down to the northern mens' prayer area. Its crowded square was dense with song, prayer, and conversation. I slipped under the archway (Wilson's Arch), found a chair just inside, and began leafing through an Israeli Bible that was written in English. When I looked up, there next to me, through a wrought-iron gate, just two or three feet away, was an Israeli soldier reading his Scriptures aloud with his M-16 draped casually downward. I remember it well. The ammunition clip was locked into the weapon. The safety was on.

I flipped through the Bible wondering if I too might find some inspiration, some spiritually rewarding experience, for this great and sacred night. Then my eyes fell on Isaiah 1, and I began to read. Chapter after chapter, page after page, Isaiah was chastising the people of Israel because they had pursued nationhood at the expense of true spiritual devotion; they had pursued national religion without pursuing the demands of justice. Isaiah spares no words: God rejects all worship, all devotion, if it is not joined to righteousness. Through the prophet, God declares:

> When you stretch out your hands [in prayer],
>   I will hide my eyes from you;
> even though you make many prayers,
>   I will not listen;
>   your hands are full of blood.
> Wash yourselves; make yourselves clean;
>   remove the evil of your doings
>   from before my eyes;
> cease to do evil,
>   learn to do good;
> seek justice,
>   rescue the oppressed,
> defend the orphan,
>   plead for the widow. (Isa. 1:15–17)

Guns and prayer were everywhere that night in Jerusalem, but no one was thinking about justice. Isaiah loved God's people, and he expected more of them. His sharp criticisms of Israel did not invalidate his commitment to them. Isaiah was not anti-Semitic. Not hardly. In fact, his commitment to the quality of Israel's nationhood was fueled by his understanding of what God wanted among his people no matter where they were.

I wish to join hands with Isaiah and in the spirit of his commitment and concern, remind Israel of its higher calling. A prophetic voice needs to be heard today in the Middle East, not an apocalyptic voice that announces the fulfillment of prophecies and the end times. Israel has strayed, and like an ox that has forgotten its master and its home, Israel has forgotten the voice of God (Isa. 1:3). I am convinced that if Isaiah were in Jerusalem today, his words would be unrelenting and his willingness to unearth Israel's sins would put his own well-being in jeopardy. Indeed, those who criticize Israel will undoubtedly be surprised at the reactions—reactions not unlike those received by the Old Testament prophets.

INTERROGATION

Ben Gurion International Airport in Tel Aviv is well-known for its security precautions for good reason. The airport has witnessed many terrible terrorist atrocities. It is fascinating while standing in line to study the design of the interior of the building and discover its hidden security precautions, from viewing windows to bomb protection. Since I was traveling alone in the spring of 1992, I knew that I would have to field the long list of questions that tourists rarely hear. My passport had far too many Israeli stamps in it. I arrived at the airport two and one-half hours before my departure home.

When I could not report to "security" that I had been residing in a typical tourist hotel and that my temporary residence had been a church hospice in Arab East Jerusalem, I quickly found that I had three security officers instead of one in front of me. "Have you talked to any Palestinians?" they asked. I mentioned that I had been traveling quite a bit interviewing Arab pastors from Galilee to Jerusalem. This comment was clearly a mistake! Then a fourth officer (apparently a supervisor) joined the group, and their conversation lapsed into Hebrew. I encouraged them to search everything I had to see that I was no security risk to the plane. But that wasn't enough. They wanted a list of Arabs whom I had talked to. My interview notes were in the attache on my shoulder, and I remarked that under no circumstances would these notes be handed over. (At this point I began to formulate some sort of lame appeal to speak with the American embassy, but I never had the opportunity to use it!) They were private (and I knew the fate of many Palestinians was at stake).

I had often heard about the "back rooms" at Ben Gurion, and many Arabs and Westerners had told me of extensive searches and questionings that went on there. I was soon to have a firsthand look. Four guards escorted me as if I were a criminal, and for ninety minutes they tore apart everything I owned, except for my notes, which stayed in my hand. It was clear that I had breached some protocol. I had been uncooperative, and now I had to pay up. Everything was stickered and dumped on the table for me to sort through. And throughout the hour and a half, young Israelis kept asking me questions about where I had been and why.

I suspected that one of the Israelis who was opening all of my toiletries was American. And so I asked him, "You're from the States, aren't you?"

He confided that he was—something about discovering his Judaism—but it was clear that he was breaking a rule by chatting with me. He looked around nervously and said he was from the East Coast. He had been in Israel for less than a year.

"This doesn't make sense, does it," I said. "We both know what this is about, tearing through my stuff."

He agreed with a furtive nod. Quietly he whispered, "These people are just afraid. And they don't know what else to do."

I pressed further, "Are you glad you're here?"

His reply was unexpected. He chuckled, shook his head in resignation, and said, "No. People back home don't know the half of this place."

NOTES

1. *New York Times*, Wednesday, June 24, 1992, A-10.
2. *New York Times*, Thursday, June 25, 1992, 1–6.
3. *Chicago Tribune*, October 11, 1992, A-6.
4. *Chicago Tribune*, October 18, 1992, 1–23.

FOUR POEMS FROM PALESTINE

RESURRECTION
(ODE ON A BURNING TANK: THE HOLY LANDS, OCTOBER 1973)
KENNETH E. BAILEY[1]

I am a voice,
   the voice of spilt blood
    crying from the land

The life is in the blood
   and for years my blood flowed in the veins of a young
man.
    My voice was heard through his voice
    and my life was his life.

Then our volcano erupted
   and for a series of numbing days
    all human voices were silenced
     amid the roar of the heavy guns,
     the harsh clank of tank tracks,
     the bone-jarring shudder of sonic booms,
      as gladiators with million-dollar swords
      killed each other high in the sky.

Then suddenly—suddenly
   there was the swish of a rocket launcher—

    a dirty yellow flash—
    and all hell roared.
The clanking of the great tracks stopped.
    My young man staggered screaming from his inferno,
    his body twitched and flopped in the sand

And I was spilt into the earth—
    into the holy earth
        of the Holy Land.

The battle moved on.
    The wounded vehicles burned,
        scorched,
            and cooled.
The "meat wagons" carried the bodies away as
    the chill of the desert night
    settled on ridge and dune,
And I stiffened and blackened in the sand.

And then—and then
As the timeless silence
    of the now scarred desert returned,
there—there congealed in the land,
    the land of prophet, priest, and king—
I heard a voice—
    a voice from an ageless age,
    a voice from other blood
        once shed violently in the land.

The voice told me this ancient story;
    precious blood intoned this ancient tale.

"A certain man had two sons.
    One was rich and the other was poor.
        The rich son had no children
        while the poor son was blessed with many sons and
daughters.

In time the father fell ill.
    He was sure he would not live through the week
    so on Saturday he called his sons to his side
        and gave each of them half of the land as their
inheritance.
        Then he died.

Before sundown the sons buried their father with respect
    as custom required.

That night the rich son could not sleep.
    He said to himself,
        'What my father did was *not just*.
        I am rich, my brother is poor.
        I have bread enough to spare,
            while my brother's children eat one day
            and trust God for the next.
    I must move the landmark which our father has set
        in the middle of the land
            so that my brother will have the greater share.
        Ah—but he must not see me.
        If he sees me he will be shamed.
        I must arise early in the morning before it is dawn
            and move the landmark!'
    With this he fell asleep
        and his sleep was secure and peaceful.

Meanwhile, the poor brother could not sleep.
    As he lay restless on his bed he said to himself,
        'What my father did was *not just*.
        Here I am surrounded by the joy of my many sons
and many daughters,
        while my brother daily faces the shame
            of having no sons to carry on his name
            and no daughters to comfort him in his old age.
    He should have the land of our fathers.
        Perhaps this will in part compensate him
        for his indescribable poverty.
    Ah—but if I give it to him he will be shamed.
    I must awake early in the morning before it is dawn
        and move the landmark which our father has set!'
    With this he went to sleep
        and his sleep was secure and peaceful.

On the first day of the week—
    very early in the morning,
    a long time before it was day,
the two brothers met at the ancient landmarker.
    They fell with tears into each others arms.
    And on that spot was built the city of Jerusalem.''

NIGHT PATROL
(AN ISRAELI SOLDIER ON THE WEST BANK)
HANAN MIKHAIL-ASHRAWI[2]

It's not the sudden hail
Of stones, nor the mocking of
Their jeers, but this deliberate
Quiet in their eyes that
Threatens to wrap itself
Around my well-uniformed
Presence and drag me into
Depths of confrontation I
Never dared probe.

Their stares bounce off stone
Walls and amateur barricades, and
I'm forced to listen
To the echo of my own
Gun fire and tear gas
Grenades in the midst of
A deafening silence which
I could almost touch, almost
But not quite.

I refuse to be made into a figment of my own
imagination. I catch
Myself, at times, catching
A glimpse of the child I
Was in one of them. That
Same old recklessness, a dare-devil
Stance, a secret wisdom that only
Youth can impart as it hurtles
Towards adulthood. Then I
begin to take substance before
My very eyes, and
Shrink back into terror as
An organism on its long
Evolutionary trek recoils at the
Touch of a human hand.

If I should once, just
Once, grasp the elusive
End of the thread which

Ties my being here with
Their being there, I
Could unravel the beginning . . . no,
No, it was not
Of will that brought me
Here, and I shall wrap myself in
Fabric woven by hands
Other than mine, perhaps
Lie down and take a nap.

Should I admit then into
My hapless dreams a thousand
Eyes, a thousand hands and allow
Unknowingly the night's
Silence to conceal me, I
Would have done no
More (no less) than what a
Thousand have done before, turn
Over in my sleep clutching my
Cocoon of army issue blankets
And hope for a different posting
In the morning.

ABSOLUTION
(TO THE FORTY WHO SHARED HUNGER FOR THIRTEEN DAYS IN JERUSALEM)
HANAN MIKHAIL-ASHRAWI[3]

You and I have shared a hunger,
beneath our makeshift tent, a
longing sharper than the spicy taut
tentacles of sizzling falafel, tighter
than the blank canopy of Arab amnesia.

We passed our abstinence from
hand to hand in reverence, examined
it in the midday heat, gritty
with the dust of our rainless summer, brittle
in the knowledge of denial.

Libations of bottled mineral
water and salt sachets were
the sacraments of our faith.

And we prayed—before the vacant
eye of the TV god we
prayed, in duplicate and triplicate
before ravenous fax machines we
prayed—until our words, along with
our lips, cracked and spilled the
mystery of blood knowledge.

In silence we traced the tracks of
scurrying insects drawing ciphers
in the dust. In silence we
marched through our via
dolorosa—kindly strangers
handing us cups of icy
water and veils with which to cover our hair—
In silence we wore the shade of a
tree by the Mosque and circled the
Holy Sepulchre then climbed the well-worn
stairs and silently went home.

We have shared a hunger and a surfeit
together until we could no longer tell
one from another, until at journey's
end I could no longer claim
mine for my own nor
surrender yours.

FROM THE DIARY OF AN ALMOST 4-YEAR-OLD
[ON RASHA HOUSHIEH OF RAMALLAH,
BLINDED BY A RUBBER BULLET]
HANNAN MIKHAIL ASHRAWI[4]

Tomorrow the bandages will come off,
I wonder, will I see half an oven? Half an apple?
Half my mother's face with my one remaining eye?
I did not see the bullet
But felt its pain exploding in my head.
This image did not disintegrate
The soldier with the big gun and steady hands
And the look in his eyes I could not understand.
If I can see him so clearly with my eyes closed,
It could be that inside our heads

We each have one spare set of eyes
To make up for the ones we lose.

Next month, on my birthday,
I'll have a brand new glass eye,
Maybe things will look round and fat in the middle.
I gaze through all my marbles.
They make the world look strange.

I hear a nine-month-old has also lost an eye,
I wonder if my soldier shot her too,
A soldier looking for litle girls who look him in the eye.
I'm old enough, almost four,
I've seen enough of life
But she's just a baby
Who didn't know any better.

NOTES

1. Kenneth E. Bailey is a New Testament scholar who was born in Egypt and has spent his entire life working in the Middle East. Fluent in Arabic, he taught for many years in Beirut and Jerusalem and now resides in Cyprus.

2. Hanan Mikhail-Ashrawi is a resident of Ramallah and professor of Medieval Literature, Bir Zeit University (see chapter 9). Printed by permission.

3. Hanan Mikhail-Ashrawi participated in a hunger strike in 1990 to protest Israeli abuses to Palestinian civil rights. This poem reflects her thoughts after the strike. Printed by permission.

4. Reprinted from *The Link* 26, no. 2 (1993): 7. Originally published in *The Middle East Justice Network*.